Devotional Introduction to Job

Devotional
Introduction to Job

by
Andrew W. Blackwood, Jr.

BAKER BOOK HOUSE
Grand Rapids, Mich.

Library of Congress Catalog Card Number: 59-15525
Copyright, 1959, by Baker Book House
Printed in the United States of America

Standard Book Number: 8010-0511-6

First printing, October 1959
Second printing, September 1970

To
C. P. B.

Acknowledgments

It would be quite impossible to thank individually the hundreds of people who, for better or worse, have helped me to bring the following essay to completion, but a few thoughts of gratitude must be expressed.

I thank the dear friend, who shall be nameless, for directing my thoughts to Job several years ago, by saying of a particular tragedy, "I don't believe that God had anything to do with it." This thought elicited a counter-thought in my mind, "If it be not He, who then is it?" My concordance did not help me to locate the line in the Bible; for the concordance maker carefully left out words like "if," "it," "be," "not," and the rest of the sentence. Vaguely I seemed to associate the idea with the Book of Job; so I had to reread the whole work for an elusive line. By the time I had located it, Job was making demands on me that would not be stilled.

I thank the congregation of the First Presbyterian Church, West Palm Beach, who bravely endured my preaching about Job for an extended period.

I thank the members of the Disciplined Order of Christ, Southeastern Area, who invited me to give the biblical talks at a retreat, thus requiring me to assemble my thoughts about Job into some sort of logical sequence. After the retreat, they showed the depth of their Christian charity by urging me to put the notes into proper form for publication.

I thank Mrs. Homer Vivian for her endless patience in retyping the manuscript, in what was supposed to be her free time.

I thank Mrs. Blackwood, and the Reverend Charles Croghan, for reading the manuscript and making valued suggestions about changes.

I thank the following named authors and publishers, for granting permission to make quotations from the works cited:

John Calvin, *Sermons from Job,* Selected and Translated by LeRoy Nixon, Wm. B. Eerdmans Publishing Company, Grand Rapids, 1952.

Mary Ellen Chase, *The Bible and the Common Reader,* Revised Edition, The Macmillan Company, New York, 1958.

Georgia Harkness, *Prayer and the Common Life,* Abingdon-Cokesbury Press, Nashville, 1948.

A. E. Housman, *The Name and Nature of Poetry,* The Macmillan Company, New York, 1933.

C. S. Lewis, *Reflections on the Psalms,* Harcourt, Brace and Company, New York, 1958.

Archibald MacLeish, "About a Trespass on a Monument," *The New York Times,* December 7, 1958.

Rudolph Otto, *The Idea of the Holy,* translated by J. W. Harvey, Oxford University Press, London, 1925.

Robert H. Pfeiffer, *Introduction to the Old Testament,* Harper, New York, 1948.

H. V. Reichert, *Job,* The Soncino Press, London, 1946.

Harrison E. Salisbury, "Communism Cannot Destroy Faith," news story in *Presbyterian Life,* September 1, 1958.

Carroll E. Simcox, *They Met at Phillippi,* Oxford University Press, Fair Lawn, New Jersey, 1958.

Richard L. Sutton and Richard L. Sutton, Jr., *Diseases of the Skin,* C. V. Mosby Company, St. Louis, 1939.

Samuel Terrien and Paul Sherer, *Job,* The Interpreters' Bible, Vol. III, The Abingdon Press, Nashville, 1954.

The Revised Standard Version of the Bible, copyrighted 1946 and 1952 by the Division of Christian Education of the National Council of Churches.

I thank the many scholars, not mentioned above, who have made a lifetime specialty of Old Testament studies, whose work has guided and benefited me. Of them all, I have found A. S. Peake most helpful, in his commentary on the Book of Job in the New Century Bible. In my general interpretation of Job, I have followed Dr. Peake. His admirers, who are many, will say that sometimes I have followed him at a considerable distance. So be it.

A small disclaimer is in order, lest I, like Elihu, exalt myself too highly. I do not pose as an Old Testament scholar.

I am a clergyman, the pastor of a medium-sized church in a medium-sized city. During the hours that a scholar would have devoted to his studies, I have been touring the valley of the shadow with my friends in (and not in) Christ. This, in its way, constitutes valid preparation for studying the Book of Job. Beyond this, I have of necessity leaned heavily upon the shoulders of those who have given their lives to the study of the Old Testament.

And, finally, I thank Cornelius Zylstra, editor, with whom I have battled (in a strictly charitable way, you understand) over every interpretation, quotation, and semi-colon in the book. His comments have been invariably helpful, though I have been somewhat variable about agreeing with them.

Those who have helped me, much as they differ in other ways, almost without exception are united in one thing. With them, I join in stating this ground of complete agreement as my reason for writing:

SOLI DEO GLORIA.

Andrew W. Blackwood, Jr.

Contents

Foreword

Ever since the man from Uz saw the kindly Light through the encircling gloom, men of good will have debated: What was the real significance of Job's life, suffering, and triumph? Many would think that after twenty-five centuries — more or less — of debate by competent scholars there would be nothing much left to say. This widespread attitude puts too much confidence in human ingenuity and gives too little recognition to the ultimate Mystery of God. Many excellent books about Job are being published each year, but the Mystery is not yet exhausted. Most of these books are written by technical experts for the benefit of clergymen. In the course of a decade or two this scholarship may well filter down to the congregations of the world, to their great spiritual enrichment. But what of today?

As I have talked with good Christian laymen during the past several years, I have discovered that the Book of Job is unknown biblical territory to most. I do not speak now of the spiritually illiterate. I am speaking about those who have a good intellectual grasp upon God's plan of salvation, who love the Bible, and show their love by reading it. Most of them have, at one time or another, read the Bible from cover to cover. So they have read every word in Job, and found there a few isolated passages they love. But it would be impossible for most to discuss in any serious detail what the Book of Job is all about. I do not anticipate that the following essay will be read by many who are not already Christians. It is my hope that it may help some Christians to appreciate a portion of the Bible that God included for their benefit.

One should approach the Book of Job with humility. It offers many traps for the wary and pitfalls for the prudent. It is filled from beginning to end with puzzles. Many of these puzzles are literary and linguistic technicalities, with which we shall not often be concerned. But many of them deal with the basic questions of Christian faith. With these we are concerned, and deeply.

I do not suggest that I have answered the questions of faith that rise from studying the Book of Job. My aim is not so exalted as that. Rather it is my hope to introduce the Christian reader to the Book of Job, giving him a map to carry along during his early explorations, after which he will need the map no more. Though I have made several comments, I have not written a commentary in any formal sense. A commentator is obliged to pick up each verse and examine it. An introducer suffers from no such requirement.

When one undertakes to study a biblical book, one is advised to ask a few questions about it. He who studies the Book of Job suffers from an abundance of contradictory answers. Competent students are not agreed even about the basic problem under discussion, much less are they agreed about the answer given, and even less than that do they agree about minor details. One who would study the literary history of Job might profitably turn to Robert H. Pfeiffer's chapter on Job in his *Introduction to the Old Testament*, pages 660-707. Dr. Pfeiffer says dryly of the many answers put forth, "The critics have suggested every possibility."

For almost every opinion expressed on the following pages, the exact opposite could easily be found, expressed by a more competent student than I. (I believe, though, that a few competent students could be found on my side of any particular fence.) This abundance of answers comes about, not because the critics are wicked or stupid, but because the Book of Job is puzzling and difficult. It deals with the ultimate Mystery, God. Mystery is not to be surveyed and precisely defined. Is it therefore useless to think about God?

The questions that one should ask about any biblical book are six: What kind of book is this? Who wrote it? Why did he write it? How does he achieve his purpose? What of the text? What of the translation?

What Kind of Book is This? It would seem a most elementary and unavoidable question: What kind of book am I dealing with? Yet the evidence is clear that many people avoid asking it when they examine a book in the Bible.

Insofar as one can classify the Book of Job, it belongs, with Proverbs and Ecclesiastes, to the Wisdom Literature in the Old Testament. These books are so-called because they were written by the wise men of old, and because they sing the praises of Wisdom. Some say that the Epistle of James, in the New Testament, should be included with Wisdom Literature. There was, of course, a tremendous volume of Wisdom Literature that is not part of our Bible.

The obvious modern counter-part of Wisdom is philosophy, which means literally "love of wisdom." But there is a decided difference. Modern philosophy means thought without presuppositions. Such thinking was unknown among the ancient Hebrew wise men, who always presupposed God and revelation. The task of Wisdom was to examine human problems in the light of faith, to penetrate ever more deeply into revelation, and to define with accuracy what is given there of divine truth and human duty.

Wisdom is a part of revelation that does not insist upon its heavenly origin. The prophets, law-givers, and priests knew a compulsion to speak as they did. "The lion hath roared, who will not fear? The Lord God hath spoken, who can but prophesy?" (Amos 3:8.) One does not sense the lion's roar echoing through the Wisdom Literature. Instead one finds observant, penetrating, kind, shrewd men looking at the world, and from the world toward God, and reaching practical conclusions. Yet these practical conclusions — the best of them at any rate — belong to the Scripture just as much as the law and the prophets. The Holy Spirit has many avenues to man's heart. Common sense, applied to an uncommon degree, is one of them.

Though the wise men of old lacked the authority of priest or prophet, there was no conflict with these other spokesmen for God. The wise men applied the truth proclaimed by priest and prophet to the problems of the day. At its best, their work was wonderfully good. Over a period of many generations, one wise man and another would toil away at the expression of some important truth or duty. The result of their labor may be examined in the Book of Proverbs, where aphorisms have been filed and polished into gems of truth that need no proof but the testimony of experience.

The path of Wisdom carried searchers far — too far. Gradually what had been a flexible inquiry into the meaning and conduct of life congealed into a rigid, intolerant system. (How many isms in the twentieth century have undergone the same hardening of the arteries?) In the Book of Job you will find Wisdom at its glorious best (e.g., chapter 28) and at its dogmatic worst (e.g., the speeches of Zophar.)

Beyond calling Job part of the Wisdom Literature, and noticing that it is a poem, further attempts to classify the book are almost hopeless. It has been called an epic, a tragedy, a drama, a didactic poem. A German critic reached the summit of confusion by describing Job as *"ein episch dramatisch Lehrgedicht."* Suitably unscrambled, that means, an epic-dramatic-didactic-poem. Each of the categories has a meaning all its own, and the Book of Job fits none of them precisely.

Mary Ellen Chase has most capably described the elusive, indefinable character of the book:

> Job is perhaps the most original work in the literature of mankind. It fits into no sphere or category. The abundance of its literary forms and of its moods and its thoughts defies any classification devised by the critics. It is not exclusively a lyric poem, nor a didactic, nor a reflective; it is all. And yet it might as well be termed a spiritual epic. Dramatic though it is in much of its movement, it is not intrinsically a drama; nor is it primarily a symposium. Nor with all its philosophy does it belong to that form of literature. All these classifications, specific or general, fail either to define or to do justice to it. It leaps the boundaries of them all to dwell in a place by itself, secure in its own peculiar and unparalleled genius.
>
> —*The Bible and the Common Reader,* page 204.

It would be almost tedious to collect the praises that have been piled upon the unique Book of Job. Thomas Carlyle said of it, "Great as the summer midnight, as the world with its sea and stars! There is nothing written, I think, in the Bible or out of it, of equal merit . . . . A noble Book; all men's Book. It is our first, oldest statement of the never-ending problem — man's destiny, and God's ways with him here in this earth" (*Lecture on Heroes*). William Blake reached his greatest heights as an artist in his interpretation of Job. Robert

Frost, in our time, has drawn upon the Job-story for *The Masque of Reason,* and Archibald MacLeish for his searching play *J. B.* What is glorious art in its own right has, down through the ages, proved a seed-idea for creative artists.

Except for the prologue and the epilogue, the introductions and a few verses in chapter 32, the Book of Job is poetry. It stands, with the work of the Psalmists, Dante, Shakespeare, Homer, and a few others at the pinnacle of the art. Our generation has produced so much gibberish, calling it poetry, that many feel a deep distaste for anything bearing the label. Many, in our time, want a sentence to say exactly what it means, and to mean exactly what it says. And this is not the case with a poem. The Psalmist sings, "The Lord is my Rock" (Psalm 18:2.) When a geologist writes about a rock, it is proper to ask him, "What kind of a rock? Sandstone? Limestone? Granite?" When the Psalmist writes about a rock, it is not wise to ask the same question.

Since the outstanding triumphs in our time have been engineering feats, some people insist upon reading the entire Bible as if it were a handbook of celestial engineering, with every statement to be taken at the same flat, exact, literal value. People who hold to this concept of the Scripture are advised to by-pass the Book of Job. They will find there many statements that cannot be taken literally.

A friend of mine used to raise what he considered a theological question from the Book of Job. He was disturbed by the hauntingly beautiful line:

When the morning stars sang together   38:7

He would point out learnedly that singing involves the operation of vocal cords and the transmission of sound waves through a medium, and "science has proved" that stars do not have vocal cords, and the reaches of outer space do not provide the type of transmitting medium that can produce sounds audible to the human ear. I would patiently answer that it did not really mean this kind of singing, and he would accuse me of saying that the Bible is untrue. I am not inventing this story. Such are the problems a clergyman must face in the twentieth century. I forebear to mention that we can now receive radio emanations from the distant stars. The poet does not refer to that type of singing either. Then what does he mean? If you do not know, I would suggest that you take a long walk, alone, in the pre-dawn darkness of a summer night, far from the nearest earthly light, and let God tell you what the line means. If any one, after that experiment, still does not understand the line, then he might as well face the fact that he does not know how to read poetry.

Since the Book of Job is great poetry, those who do not believe in God still may appreciate and enjoy the poem for its literary value. Indeed, they sometimes tell us that their appreciation is on a much higher level than that of us who believe; for we are appreciating the theological message, and they are reveling in the poetry for its own sake. I have asked a number of such aesthetes why a poet bothers to include a meaning, if he does not want his readers to notice. Though the answer has sometimes been quite extended, I have never understood it. A. E. Housman, an atheist, said:

> If a man is insensible to poetry, it does not follow that he gets no pleasure from poems. Poems very seldom consist of poetry and nothing else; and pleasure can be derived from their ingredients. I am convinced that most readers, when they think they are admiring poetry, are deceived by inability to analyze their sensations, and that they are really admiring, not the poetry of the passage before them, but something else in it, which they like better than poetry... Good religious poetry, whether in Keble, or Dante, or Job is likely to be most justly appreciated and most discriminatingly relished by the undevout.
>
> —*The Name and Nature of Poetry*, pages 32, 33.

If, as Mr. Housman seems to be saying, one should disagree with a poem really to appreciate it, then the Christian reader will find much to appreciate in the Book of Job.

There are, unquestionably, poetic values in Job that one can relish without regard to one's religious beliefs. And there are, unquestionably, religious values in Job that one can relish without regard to one's appreciation of poetry in general. But surely we must recognize that the Holy Spirit saw fit to incorporate these two sets of values into one work. The Christian attitude toward religious poetry, particularly that found in the Bible, has been well expressed by C. S. Lewis, an atheist who became a Christian.

> Those who talk of reading the Bible "as literature" sometimes mean, I think, reading it without attending to the main thing it is about.... That seems to me to be nonsense. But there is a saner sense in which the Bible, since it is after all literature, cannot properly be read except as literature; and the different parts of it as the different sorts of literature they are. Most emphatically the Psalms must be read as poems; as lyrics, with all the license and all the formalities, the hyperboles, the emotional rather than logical connections, which are proper to lyric poetry. They must be read as poems if they are to be understood, no less than French must be read as French or English as English. Otherwise we shall miss what is in them and think we see what is not.
>
> —*Reflections on the Psalms,* page 3.

Poetry is the language of imagination and intuition. Poetry penetrates to a depth in the human soul that reason and logic can never reach. Poetry achieves its effects, as Mr. Lewis has suggested, by casting away the shackles of orderly prose, and developing new freedoms of its own. In reading Christian poetry, one must not treat it as if it were Christian prose. When the Joban poet speaks about the morning stars singing together, one must appreciate what he means, and not reduce what is glorious to the level of silliness.

Who Wrote This Book? Sometimes the question of authorship is more important than at others. For example, when the opening line in a biblical book tells me that the Apostle Paul wrote it, and a critic tells me that the Apostle Paul did not write the book, I wish to be convinced by weighty evidence before accepting the conclusion. In this case, I would consider the question of authorship extremely important. In the case of Job, however, it would seem to me of comparatively little importance, as far as our appreciation is concerned. Who wrote Job? The question is unanswerable, though I have read a book that took sixty-two pages to say so.

We can but guess the century in which the Book of Job was composed. The Talmud suggests in one place that Moses was the author. This suggestion is not widely accepted today. On the following page other authors are nominated, ranging from the time of the Judges down to the time of King Ahasuerus. For myself, I incline slightly toward the belief that the first edition of Job was composed during, or shortly after, the Babylonian captivity of the Hebrews. Thus the epic of a suffering man was wrung from the heart of a suffering nation. There are various bits of scattered evidence pointing toward this conclusion. One of them is the comparison between Job 3:1-12 and Jeremiah 20:14-18. If you will examine these carefully, you will decide it probable that this portion of Job was written after Jeremiah's time.

There is good reason to believe that there were several authors, rather than one; that the Book was composed over a period of generations, or perhaps centuries, before it reached its present form. A few vocal Christians think that one is tampering with God's holy Word when one makes such a suggestion. Quite the contrary. There is nothing inherently wicked about trying to learn how a book in the Bible was written. Though some higher critics have committed masterpieces of nonsense, their task of examining the biblical text, and trying to reach some tenable conclusions, is implicit in respect for the divine message. The correct antidote for bad criticism is good criticism, not closing one's eyes to the problems.

Job is part of the Wisdom Literature in the Old Testament. We know that Proverbs had many human authors; for we have the names of several. Most critics today believe that Ecclesiastes was a joint product, though they have yet to convince me. And practically all agree that several authors produced Job. There are three chief reasons for thinking that Job had more than one author. One finds several different styles of writing. Different approaches to the mystery of faith are found. There are serious breaks in the logical continuity. The simplest, hence most probable, explanation for these differences is that we have in Job the product of several human authors. In the literature today, these authors are lumped together under the massively ugly title "the Joban poet." For want of a better term, I shall use it, occasionally.

If there were many authors of Job, then there must have been at least one editor who finally assembled the different parts into the masterpiece we have today. This man is among the outstanding geniuses in literary history, yet today he is heartily condemned and criticized by most who write about Job. People who write about Job are, by definition, authors.

Authors as a class are likely to view editors as a class with a cold and critical eye. It is our way of getting even.

As early as the twelfth century, the Jewish scholar Raschi suggested that 27:11ff was spoken by one of the comforters rather than by Job. Last century many students, particularly in Germany, practically rewrote the Book of Job in their zeal to undo the editor's work and recover what they believed was the author's original intent. They showed more ingenuity than plausibility. By a process of declaring many sections "spurious" one critic even demonstrated that Job is an atheistic tract.

By now, practically everybody who has studied the matter agrees that we do not have today the first draft of Job. Many have undertaken to restore the first draft. For example, Dr. James Moffatt, in his translation, and Dr. J. M. Powis Smith, in *An American Translation,* have made some major re-arrangements, recovering what possibly was the original order of several passages. Yet, as one reads the Book of Job in its present form, it is hard to think that the editor failed. It is quite possible that he toned down some of Job's more rash remarks, though it is hard to imagine anything more rash than some that remain. It is quite possible that the editor changed the position of certain verses, for reasons we do not know today. But when the work left his hand, it was what Alfred Lord Tennyson called, "the greatest poem, whether of ancient or of modern time."

Undue preoccupation with human authorship may well lead one to overlook the divine Author. In the last analysis, the Holy Spirit wrote the Book of Job. He may have worked through many human minds in producing one inspired book. The plurality of authorship would seem to me a question of literary, rather than religious, importance. I believe that God speaks today through the Book of Job. I believe that He exposes many basic errors in modern thought through this book. I believe that He has helped me, through my reading Job. And I believe that He will help you, if you read it thoughtfully. No one is likely ever to reach more than a tentative conclusion about the question of human authorship. Does it really matter, as long as the Voice from the Whirlwind still resounds?

Why Was the Book Written? Nine Christians out of ten will tell you that Job was written to explain why the righteous suffer. True enough, the book is full of just such explanation. In wearisome repetition Job's comforters announce that the righteous do not suffer. Suffering comes as a punishment for sin. The righteous receive blessings from the hand of God. Sinners receive the punishment they so richly deserve. This belief is known as the doctrine of material retributive justice. It is a simplification of a profound and important truth. Sometimes, when something profoundly true is over-simplified, it becomes profoundly false. The author of Job presents the doctrine of material retributive justice only to refute it.

The prophets of Israel had proclaimed that God rules the world in justice. Ezekiel, with his famous dictum, "The soul that sinneth, it shall die" (Ezekiel 18:4) applied divine justice not only to the nation but to the individual. The wise men who wrote the Book of Proverbs stressed the connection between godliness and true success in this world. From these divinely revealed truths had grown a comfortable faith that virtue is always rewarded and evil is always punished. This faith has seen a remarkable resurgence in the mid-twentieth century, even among Christians who look to the Crucified. Christians ought also to notice that evil persons frequently prosper.

The Book of Job refutes the idea of material retributive justice. The author suggests in several places that pain has an educative purpose. He does not refute this suggestion with the same vigor that he saves for the doctrine of retribution. But few could say that the Book of Job was written to discuss the disciplinary value of pain.

I have read, with more amazement than profit, a book attempting to show that Job sets an example of the way a Christian should endure pain. The Book of Job is glorious because it shows people acting the way people act, rather than the way we ought to act. Job is querulous, antagonistic, bitter and despondent by turn. Surely in this Job does not set a good example. It is only as faith triumphs over despair that the example is set.

The Book of Job deals with a problem deeper even than the problem of pain. It is the answer to the Satan's cynical question,

Doth Job fear God for nought?   1:9

Why does man worship? Why does the prayer of faith rise from hovels as well as from mansions? Do we love God because of His gifts, or because He is God? These are the questions answered in the Book of Job.

A friend of mine lost four daughters in one night. He faced the tragedy with dignity and courage — there was no alternative. But in the valley of the shadow he accepted faith in Christ as the active principle of his life. Before the loss, in his time of blessing, he had been merely a nominal Christian. Anyone can understand and appreciate the dignity and courage. But many will ask, Why the faith? After God took away so much, how could this man trust Him?

We who enjoy the blessings of political liberty ought daily to thank God for them. In actual practice, sometimes we tend to take for granted what our fathers have earned at great cost. It would be understandable if faith were widespread among the free, well-fed, prosperous peoples in the world. Now look at Russia, where an estimated 50,000,000 people are practicing Christians, almost none of whom have ever known anything but the Communist government. I quote Harrison E. Salisbury, one of America's foremost authorities on the Soviet Union, Pulitzer Prize winning correspondent. I believe that his opinion is more likely to be accurate than that of some who speak with louder voices.

> Communism cannot destroy faith. Persecution may cost the Church many temporal possessions, but it deepens and strengthens the role of religion and belief in God in the masses of people... The Russian Church, having endured persecution of every kind, has survived and is today growing because of its deep spiritual roots, because it is serving its people, and because its faith has been purified by the sufferings it has undergone.
>
> —*Presbyterian Life,* Sept. 1, 1958.

"Its faith has been purified by the sufferings it has undergone." To many, these sufferings seem a direct proof that the faith is mistaken, that God is not justice, mercy, and love.

Certainly the Soviet Union has done everything possible to eliminate faith. For all of the 50,000,000 it is inexpedient, for some it is physically dangerous, and for many it has meant torture and death to profess Jesus Christ. So the Church grows. Why?

I have heard many say, "Money is the most important thing there is." Job lost his money.

I have heard many say, "Love is the greatest of all blessings." Job lost his children. His wife deserted him, spiritually. The people of his community turned against him. Those who came to comfort stayed to torture him. Job lost all he had known of earthly love.

Not long ago a chronic invalid said to me, "Nothing is more important than health." Job lost his health.

With these staggering losses piled atop each other, Job almost lost his faith; until the Voice from the Whirlwind cried that, though Job had lost his grip on God, God had not lost His grip on Job.

Why does man worship? One Sunday after Church a good Christian friend, shuddering slightly, handed me a letter he had recently received:

GOOD LUCK PRAYER

Trust in the Lord with all thine heart. I'll always acknowledge him and he will direct thy faith. This prayer has been around the world four times and the one that broke the chain had bad luck. The original came from the Netherlands. The luck of it has been sent to you, you are to have good luck four days after receiving it by mail. Please copy this and see what happens four days after receiving it. Do not send money and please don't keep this copy, just send this copy and four others to people you wish to have good luck, it must leave your hands 24 hours after you receive it.

This letter bears the names of twenty people. I wish that I could believe the whole thing a practical joke in deplorable taste, but I fear that I must accept it at face value. At least twenty people in the world of our time follow the teaching of the unnamed Dutch theologian that we pray in order to be lucky.

Why does man worship? One would gather from the bulk of twentieth-century religious literature that religion is the one-way road to health, prosperity, peace of mind, success, freedom from inhibitions, and an integrated personality. The

Book of Job suggests that our faith was designed to be an approach to God, who in Himself is worth far more than all His gifts put together.

In the valley of the shadow, Job had a religious experience. This convinced him of God's reality, power, and concern. Though his friends could not argue him into faith, God led him to believe. God works not only through the rational intellect; He works through our senses and feelings, our imaginations and our intuitions, through every means of human cognition, including the unconscious. Few can describe analytically the way they come into faith, but a considerable number do arrive there. Job, the doubter, sitting in the ashes, sensed the *mysterium tremendum,* and he believed once more. As Rudolph Otto, one of the most influential religious thinkers in the twentieth century, has so aptly expressed it:

> We are dealing with something for which there is only one appropriate expression, *mysterium tremendum.* The feeling of it may at times come sweeping like a gentle tide, pervading the mind with a tranquil mood of deepest worship. It may pass over into a more set and lasting attitude of the soul, continuing, as it were, thrillingly vibrant and resonant, until at last it dies away and the soul resumes its "profane," non-religious mood of everyday experience. It may burst in sudden eruption up from the depths of the soul with spasms and convulsions, or lead to the strangest excitements, to intoxicated frenzy, to transport, and to ecstasy. It has its wild and demonic forms and can sink to an almost grisly horror and shuddering. It has its crude, barbaric antecedents and early manifestations, and again it may be developed into something beautiful and pure and glorious. It may become the hushed, trembling, and speechless humility of the creature in the presence of—whom or what? In the presence of that which is a *Mystery* inexpressible and above all creatures.

> —*The Idea of the Holy,* pages 12, 13.

God is the answer to Job's questions; not some propositions logically arranged, but God. If, perchance, you think Him an inadequate answer, then the Book of Job is not for you. Those who have known God believe that such knowledge is better by far than anything that the world can give or take away. Job found it so.

How Does the Author Achieve His Purpose? The Holy Spirit brought the Book of Job into being. We have seen good rea-

sons for believing that the Holy Spirit worked through the
lives of several human authors in producing the one inspired
Book. In other words, the Book has a human side that we
can examine profitably, as long as we remember that we are
discussing the way in which the Spirit of the living God brings
a particular message to the world.

Most critics who have thought deeply about the Book of
Job agree that the poet retold, in terms of his day, the story
of Job, much as Archibald MacLeish, in our time, has retold
it in his play *J. B.*

There has been much argument, whether the Book of Job
describes a historical character or if it is a parable. The Holy
Spirit used the parable widely in the New Testament. I
should not wonder at His using it in the Old. Having said
this, I shall declare that in my fallible opinion, Job was a
historical character who lived in the land of Uz and suffered
most bitterly before his final victory.

I believe that Job was a historical character. However, the
value in the Book of Job lies in its worth as a parable, not in
its accuracy as a chronicle. A chronicle reports a particular
set of events. A parable exposes a universal truth. The parable may or may not be based upon historical fact.

I daresay Jesus drew upon fact for His Parable of the Prodigal Son. He recalled a village tragedy from His boyhood in
Nazareth, and retold it in a manner that gave the particular
incident a universal dimension. Does it really matter if I
am mistaken in my supposition? We have the parable today. That is what counts, not its antecedents. Just so, we
have the Book of Job. I think that it reflects a historical
event, though I may be badly mistaken. In any case, one's
reason for reading Job is not to learn about social customs and
religious beliefs in ancient Uz. One reads instead for the
universal message of grace mediated through pain.

Even the most staunch literalist must agree that the Book
of Job — if it depicts history at all — shows the events as they
have been interpreted through an artist's mind. For example,
one looks at the symbolic number of cattle and sheep, sons
and daughters. At the end, most of these symbolic numbers
are precisely doubled. One is transported to a heavenly court,
where God engages in a transaction that to take literally

would be sheer blasphemy, though as a symbol the transaction is profound. But most telling of all is the language itself. This is not a literal report of actual conversations. People do not talk in magnificent poetry.

Though the Book of Job is thoroughly Hebraic in its outlook, Job himself is not represented as ,being an Israelite. (After all, there were no Israelites until the time of Jacob.) The key elements of Hebrew faith, the Law and the Temple, are missing. The sacred name Yahweh is found but rarely. The land of Uz where Job dwelt is a half-fabulous area, vaguely somewhere to the east of Palestine, north of Edom, in or near the Arabian Desert, definitely not part of the Holy Land. (Note Lamentations 4:21.) Job is described consistently as an Arabian prince.

Establishing dates for Job is even more hopeless than locating Uz on a map. Apparently he lived in the patriarchal age, but this gives us a leeway of a millennium, one way or another. Yet, at this completely unknown time, in this almost unknown place, lived a righteous man who suffered. He became a folk-hero in Israel. We find him mentioned only once in the Old Testament outside the book that bears his name. The other mention is Ezekiel 14:14f, where Job is ranked with Noah and Daniel, both in righteousness and as a master of intercessory prayer. Since, probably, the Book of Job was written in large part to refute a cheap and shallow interpretation of Ezekiel's prophecy, one may legitimately draw a few inferences: Job lived, suffered, and triumphed. The story of his agony and ultimate blessing was told and retold around the campfires on a thousand hills, over a period of perhaps a thousand years. Gradually the story crystallized into a traditional form that was hallowed by centuries of repetition. The hero's name became part of a proverb, "The patience of Job." Ezekiel refers to this folk-hero in his prophecy. The Joban poet was led by the Holy Spirit to take the Job-story as the framework for his examination into the eternal why of faith. The traditional prose forms the prologue and the epilogue. The heart of the Book is the poem, which Mary Ellen Chase calls, "The incomparable literary masterpiece of our Bible" (*The Bible and the Common Reader,* p. 204).

The interpretation of Job's literary origins, as described here, is widely accepted today. To me it seems the most probable explanation for the human side of divine revelation. As far as the major purpose of Job is concerned, the solution to literary problems is relatively unimportant. Our purpose in reading Job is to consider God's way with man, not to solve a literary puzzle.

What of the Text? The question is technical. Any serious answer must delve into technicalities that are far beyond the scope of this book. Even if I were able to discuss such matters, the lay reader would not be able to follow the discussion.

Suffice it to say, in the days when books were copied by hand it was inevitable that errors were made in the copying. The next copyist, like as not, would copy the error. So, in the course of a few centuries, a manuscript might vary considerably from the author's intent. Once I said something of the sort in public, and an irritated Christian (who had not yet heard about the virtue of charity) loudly accused me of saying that the Bible is a tissue of lies. Whether it fits in with one's theology or not, the fact is inescapable that manuscript A has one reading, and manuscript B has another, and the inference is simply unavoidable that both cannot be what the author wrote. Job's comforters would have found some way out of the dilemma; they were wonderful at explaining away facts they did not like. But we who are less gifted must acknowledge an unpleasant fact when we see it. The unpleasant fact is, we cannot always be sure exactly what the Joban poet wrote.

Among the Jewish people centuries ago the textual problem was acute. Rabbi X quoted the Scripture as saying this, and Rabbi Y appealed to the same passage and found it quite differently worded. So a group of scholars called the Masoretes, beginning about the seventh century of the Christian era, worked to bring order out of confusion. In addition to reconciling the divergent readings, the Masoretes provided vowels, a luxury their predecessors had scorned. By and large, the Masoretic text is excellent. Scholars disagree with this or that interpretation, but all hold high esteem for the men who labored, long ago, to set God's word free from human error.

In the third century B. C., the Hebrew community in Alexandria wished a Bible in their own tongue, which happened to be Greek. The translation that resulted is called the Septuagint (abbreviated LXX) from the tradition that seventy translators prepared it. Obviously, if this were an accurate translation, it would give much help to the textual student. However, the Jewish scholars in the third century B.C. were not so deeply concerned about precise wordings as were their successors in the seventh century A.D. The Septuagint is an invaluable aid, but one must not rely upon it blindly.

With this much introduction to the subject, I yield the floor to an expert, Samuel Terrien:

> It is to be expected that an ancient writing composed in highly original poetry and presenting many unusual words and grammatical constructions, several repetitions of motifs in various garbs, a style which cultivates subtleties of expression bordering sometimes on the esoteric, and more especially a theological outlook which could never become popular, would suffer at the hand of pedestrian editors and copyists. To say that the Hebrew text of Job is not well preserved is therefore an understatement. Yet the fact that it was preserved at all deserves recognition. Lower critics have done considerable research on the Joban text, although it must be added that some of them have wrought more damage even than censorious editors and careless scribes have done in the early years of transmission.
>
> Scrutiny of the Masoretic Text and comparison with the ancient versions, especially that of the Septuagint, have revealed a number of graphic errors, particularly omissions of letters, words, and lines, as well as some transpositions. However, the critic should be slow to tamper with the text without due warrant. Modern discoveries, especially in the field of comparative linguistics, have proved more than once that a strange form or supposedly "faulty spelling" had been rightly preserved by the Masoretes. Moreover, the testimony of the versions, especially that of the Septuagint, is not always helpful, for the Alexandrine and other translators often paraphrased and sometimes deliberately corrected the wording and the ideas of the original in order to elucidate an obscure passage or even to impose a theological bias.
>
> —*The Interpreter's Bible,* Volume III, *Job,* pages 896, 897.

In what follows, I have heeded Dr. Terrien's admonition to proceed with caution in regard to tampering with the Masoretic Text. The Masoretes may not have recovered the

Joban poet's words precisely; but they came much closer than
I ever could.

What of the Translation? This question, too, is technical.
Those who know nothing of the problems involved sometimes have firmly held opinions about the matter. Translation is hard work. The Book of Job is, in many ways, the
hardest book in the entire Bible for the translator. Shall he
give an exact, literal rendering of the Hebrew? If he does, no-
body except another Hebrew scholar will understand it. Shall
he express in modern English what he thinks the author intended to convey? Then he is parting from God's holy Word.

Every new Biblical translation has been roundly criticized
and abused by those who love the dictions, cadences, and even
the errors, in the old. For example, when the Authorized
Version was published in 1611, Hugh Broughton, the most
competent British Hebraist of his time, wrote, "Tell His
Majesty that I had rather be rent in pieces with wild horses
than any such translation, by my consent, should be urged
on poor churches" (quoted in *The English Bible and its
Story,* by Hugh Baikie, page 301). There may have been a
touch of sour grapes in the attitude. Broughton's temper was
such that he had not been included in the company of translators. Of course such considerations would be unthinkable
in the twentieth century, when all criticism of new translations
is conducted in a spirit of humility and charity.

For myself, I believe that the best translation of Job is
the Authorized — or King James — Version. This statement
must be qualified. In recent centuries, Hebrew scholars have
improved upon some interpretations. The English language
has undergone many changes since 1611. Some verses that
were crystal clear then are opaque today. With all my ad-
miration for the Authorized Version, still I urge one approach-
ing Job for the first time to read the Revised Standard Version,
since it is much easier reading for the modern person. The
Book of Job presents quite enough problems without adding a language difficulty. Yet, with these disclaimers before
me, I believe that the Authorized Version of Job is the best
English translation; for it is majestic poetry in its own right.
Other translations, each with its own excellence, fall short
in this regard. The Revised Standard Version reaches to the

mind more readily than does the Authorized. But the older translation sings its way into the heart. Since Job is, after all, a poem and not a theological dissertation, to my thinking the translation that is the best poetry is the best.

The quotations that follow are taken from the Authorized Version, with occasional modifications to clarify the meaning. To illustrate why modification was thought necessary, the Authorized Version reads:

> Who hath prevented Me, that I should repay
> him?   41:11

To many readers, the remark might just as well have been left in the original Hebrew. The word "prevent" has changed its meaning during the centuries since 1611. Though it is desirable to retain the stately cadence of post-Elizabethan English, it is even more desirable to communicate with the reader. Since the Hebrew verb implies "precede with a gift," the verse as here translated reads:

> Who hath given Me a gift that I should repay him?   41:11

Then there are such matters as the term "its" where the Authorized Version invariably reads "his," and the complete absence of quotation marks. Respect for a classic does not preclude an occasional stylistic change from an ancient usage that today is merely annoying.

In a very few instances it is believed that the translators in 1611 were mistaken. Outstanding among these instances is 13:15, possibly the most quoted verse from the Book of Job. Here the translators followed a marginal note in the Masoretic Text, rather than the Text itself.

On the flyleaf of the Authorized Version you read that this work was "with the former translations diligently compared and revised." I have reversed this procedure in making comparison chiefly with later translations. Of these, three have been especially helpful, the American Revised Version (1901), that made by the Jewish Publication Society of America (1917), and the Revised Standard Version (1952).

A question that has plagued all translators concerns the apparatus of technical scholarship. In the Authorized Version, for instance, when the translators thought it necessary to insert a word to clarify a meaning, they italicized the insert.

The American Revised Version has voluminous footnotes, of tremendous value to the Hebrew student, though of more limited usefulness to the general reader. The Revised Standard Version has occasional footnotes, and frequent reminders — in Job at least — that the Hebrew is obscure. Since this essay is designed as a devotional introduction to Job, it was decided to omit such matters. For example, one passage, where the Authorized Version is obscure, reads here:

> Ye say, "God layeth up iniquity for his children!"   21:19
> Let Him reward the wicked himself,
>   that he may know it.

The words "ye say" and "the wicked," the capitalized "H", and the quotation marks are additions. It is believed that they clarify the meaning. Without them one is bogged down in a morass of pronouns. But why put in a footnote to say all this?

The general rule followed has been to call no attention to a change in translation, unless it involves a change in meaning from that found in the Authorized Version. Those who walk with assurance through the dark mysteries of Hebrew grammar will understand the reason for any modification, whether or not they agree with me. Those who do not read Hebrew would find my defense of most particular translations to be gibberish.

I am not writing for the benefit of Hebrew scholars. Certainly I do not include myself in their ranks. Scholars will know where to turn for technical analysis in plenty. What follows is a discussion of a work that was designed to be read, not by scholars alone, but by all who love God. Unhappily, when the lover of God turns to a book about Job, he usually finds himself swamped in a deluge of technicalities even more baffling than the message of Job. At an inevitable sacrifice in precision, I have left out practically all of the technicalities.

I. PROLOGUE IN PROSE 1:1–2:13

A. Introduction of Job 1:1-5

B. The first testing 1:6-22
   1. The council in Heaven 1:6-12
     a. God's confidence in Job 1:6-8
     b. The Satan's challenge to God 1:9-12
   2. The first afflictions 1:13-22
     a. The messengers 1:13-19
     b. The faith of Job 1:20-22

C. The second testing 2:1-10
   1. The second council in Heaven 2:1-6
     a. God's confidence in Job 2:1-3
     b. The Satan's second challenge to God 2:4-6
   2. The second afflictions 2:7-10
     a. The sickness 2:7-8
     b. Job's wife 2:9
     c. Job's faith 2:10

D. The comforters 2:11-13

Prologue in Prose 1:1—2:13

> There was a man in the land of Uz whose name
> was Job;   1:1

The word "man" has two meanings. Sometimes it means the
entire human race, sometimes it means a single member of
the race. The opening words in the Book of Job suggest
forcibly that the ensuing discussion will concern one individual, but through his experiences the reader will examine the
problems of Everyman. We have noted in the Foreword that
the land of Uz was a half-mythical area lying beyond the
boundaries of the Holy Land. The name of the man who
lived there may have had a symbolic meaning at one ·time.
That time has long since passed by. This is one reason for
believing that Job was a historical character. Were the following narrative a myth, probably the characters would have
significant names. But historical characters play out life's
brief drama without much regard for the etymological im-
port of their names. Job was a man who represents Everyman to us. The story of Job has a universal dimension.

To the man from Uz came many blessings, chief among
them a large and happy family, the respect of his neighbors,
material wealth, and a firm, intelligent faith in God. Though
I believe Job to be a historical character, I believe that we
are not reading literal history in the description of his riches.
The numbers three, five, seven, and ten, with their multiples,
have a religious rather than a bookkeeping significance. They
indicate complete sufficiency.

The man from Uz was blameless, not "perfect" as in the
Authorized Version; for to the ancient Hebrew perfection
could be ascribed to God alone. Christians have troubled
themselves quite needlessly about this, raising a question that
almost certainly never occurred to the Joban poet. Christians believe that Jesus, and only Jesus, has led a completely

35

blameless life on earth. His purity of life did not exempt
Him from cruel suffering. Job was not sinless in the same
sense that Jesus was sinless, but he was a righteous, devout
man.

> That man was blameless and upright, and one that   1:1
> feared God, and eschewed evil. And there were   1:2
> born unto him seven sons and three daughters. His   1:3
> substance also was seven thousand sheep, and three
> thousand camels, and five hundred yoke of oxen, and
> five hundred she-asses, and a very great household;
> so that this man was the greatest of all the men of
> the east.

Among Job's many blessings was an unusual degree of
harmony within his large family. One gathers that it was
unusual in the ancient east for daughters to share in their
brothers' festivity.

The narrator shows Job offering sacrifice for his children,
lest they be guilty of secret sin in their thoughts. Thus
we see sketched in a few lines the picture of a man at the
peak of his vigorous maturity, outstanding in ability, successful in the always-difficult task of raising a family, who recognizes that faith in God is concerned with the inward dis-
position, not merely with outward rituals and ceremonies.
If anyone deserves to be at peace with God and man, Job does.

> And his sons went and feasted in their houses, every   1:4
> one his day; and sent and called for their three
> sisters to eat and to drink with them. And it was so, 1:5
> when the days of their feasting were gone about,
> that Job sent and sanctified them, and rose up early
> in the morning, and offered burnt offerings accord-
> ing to the number of them all: for Job said, "It
> may be that my sons have sinned, and cursed God
> in their hearts." Thus did Job continually.

The scene shifts from earth to heaven, where the sons of
God are presenting themselves before the Lord, like courtiers
rendering an account of their stewardship to the king. Among
the sons of God, but presumably not one of them, is the
Satan. At this stage of religious history, Satan is not yet
a proper name. It is a title, meaning "The Adversary."

Since the Satan does not appear in the following poem, it is not needful here to examine into all that Satan meant and has subsequently meant in religious history.

God challenges the Satan, asking him to consider Job, a blameless, upright man, and the Adversary retorts with a question upon which all the succeeding discussion hinges. Since he cannot well deny Job's piety, the Satan casts doubt upon his motives.

> Now there was a day when the sons of God came 1:6
> to present themselves before the Lord, and the
> Satan came also among them. And the Lord said 1:7
> unto the Satan, "Whence comest thou?" Then the
> Satan answered the Lord, and said, "From going
> to and fro in the earth, and from walking up and
> down in it." And the Lord said unto the Satan, 1:8
> "Hast thou considered my servant Job, that there
> is none like him in the earth, a blameless and an
> upright man, one that feareth God, and escheweth
> evil?" Then the Satan answered the Lord, and 1:9
> said, "Doth Job fear God for nought? Hast not 1:10
> thou made an hedge about him, and about his
> house, and about all that he hath on every side?
> Thou hast blessed the work of his hands, and his
> substance is increased in the land: but put forth 1:11
> Thine hand now, and touch all that he hath, and
> he will curse Thee to Thy face."

Here rises the first, and in many ways the most difficult, theological puzzle in the Book of Job. God makes an agreement with the Satan. Many commentators have described this agreement as a bet. God gives the Satan permission to strip away all of Job's possessions. If there is any who thinks this a literal description of the way God deals with man, at this point he and I must part company. The agreement symbolizes the power of evil in human life. Calling a thing a symbol is not dismissing its importance. The power of evil is the dread reality with which Christians must constantly live.

Why did God permit the Satan to have power over Job? Turning back to the origins of human history, why did God permit our first ancestors to be tempted? On the larger scale, why is the power of evil regnant in the world today? I do not know. I am not privileged to read the divine Mind. Examining the Book of Job with some care has not helped me a bit in answering these inescapable questions of faith. But this one thing I know: We do not suffer and grieve because God and the devil made a bet with our souls as the stake on the table. The agreement is a symbol of that which we do not, and perhaps cannot, understand.

Insofar as the Book of Job answers the Why of suffering, the answer is mystery. The Voice from the Whirlwind asks man to recognize his ignorance before the mystery of creation, and to trust in God when he does not understand. The agreement in the opening verses is a powerful symbolic device, designed to drive home that God's dealing with man is often mysterious to man.

> And the Lord said unto the Satan, "Behold, all that   1:12
> he hath is in thy power; only upon himself put
> not forth thine hand." So the Satan went forth from
> the presence of the Lord.

In swift and horrible succession calamities came upon Job: the loss of his herd to marauders; the flock's destruction by lightning; the theft of his camels; and then the ultimate blow, the death of his children in a hurricane.

> And there was a day when his sons and his daugh-   1:13
> ters were eating and drinking wine in their eldest
> brother's house: and there came a messenger unto   1:14
> Job, and said, "The oxen were plowing, and the
> asses feeding beside them; And the Sabeans fell   1:15
> upon them, and took them away; yea, they have
> slain the servants with the edge of the sword; and
> I only am escaped alone to tell thee." While he was   1:16
> yet speaking, there came also another, and said,
> "The fire of God is fallen from heaven, and hath
> burned up the sheep, and the servants, and con-
> sumed them; and I only am escaped alone to tell
> thee." While he was yet speaking, there came also   1:17
> another, and said, "The Chaldeans made out three
> bands, and fell upon the camels, and have carried

them away, yea, and slain the servants with the edge
of the sword; and I only am escaped alone to tell
thee." While he was yet speaking, there came also   1:18
another, and said, "Thy sons and thy daughters
were eating and drinking wine in their eldest
brother's house: and, behold, there came a great   1:19
wind from the wilderness, and smote the four
corners of the house, and it fell upon the young
men, and they are dead; and I only am escaped
alone to tell thee."

Job made the outward signs of mourning that were cus-
tomary in his day, and uttered his unsurpassed statement of
resignation. In the first of many deviations from our ideas
about poetic construction, the Joban poet introduces the
glorious climax of faith at the beginning rather than at the
end of his work. It is Job's ultimate triumph that he regains
the triumphant faith expressed thus early in his sorrows.

Job's attitude is called resignation. Properly understood,
resignation is an outstanding Christian virtue. Unhappily,
what is noble can be, and often has been, abused. The Com-
munists delight in pointing out times when Christians have
urged the poor to accept their lot with humility, rather
than working to change a rotten situation. Indeed, I once
heard an alleged Christian attack a slum-clearance measure,
not on the ground that it was a poor measure (as it was)
but on the ground that God wants people to rot away in
slums. After all, Jesus said, "The poor always ye have with
you" (John 12:8.) Such heroic acceptance of other people's
anguish is contemptible. Job, in his days of vigor, would
have none of it, as you can discover by reading chapters
29-31, where Job says, among other things:

I brake the jaws of the wicked,   29:17
    and plucked the spoil out of his teeth.

When Job was in a position to combat evil, he combatted
it, thus expressing his faith. But now he is faced with evils
he cannot overcome; so, like a man of faith, he accepts.

Almost certainly you have heard the prayer that I learned
from some members of Alcoholics Anonymous. Since learn-
ing it, I have heard it attributed to thinkers as diverse as

Reinhold Niebuhr and Norman Vincent Peale. Whoever composed it, it is a cry for help that I utter with considerable frequency:

> Almighty God, give me strength to change those things
>   that ought to be changed,
>   and grace to accept those things that cannot be changed,
>   and sense enough to tell the difference.

When Job had the strength, he worked at changing the things that ought to be changed. Now he is faced with a situation that cannot be changed, and he accepts it in faith. He does not understand, but he trusts God.

> Then Job arose, and rent his mantle, and shaved   1:20
> his head, and fell down upon the ground, and wor-
> shiped, and said, "Naked came I out of my mother's   1:21
> womb, and naked shall I return thither: the Lord
> gave, and the Lord hath taken away; blessed be
> the name of the Lord." In all this Job sinned not,   1:22
> nor charged God foolishly.

When the sons of God gather before the divine throne once more, the Satan is again with them. The Lord reiterates His confidence in Job, and the Satan answers with the cryptic words, "Skin for skin." Possibly this is a proverb that suggested more to readers in another day than to us. One Rabbi has ingeniously translated the expression, "There is a skin beneath the skin." That is, only the surface has been scratched. The Satan's implication is quite clear, Job's integrity has not been proved. Job is still serving God for the reward of physical health, rather than for love of God. The Lord accepts the second challenge, and permits the Satan to afflict Job with physical pain, though he is not permitted to take Job's life.

> Again there was a day when the sons of God came   2:1
> to present themselves before the Lord, and the Satan
> came also among them, to present himself before
> the Lord. And the Lord said unto the Satan,   2:2
> "From whence comest thou?" And the Satan an-
> swered the Lord, and said, "From going to and fro
> in the earth, and from walking up and down in it."

> And the Lord said unto the Satan, "Hast thou con- 2:3
> sidered My servant Job, that there is none like him
> in the earth, a blameless and an upright man, one
> that feareth God, and escheweth evil? And still he
> holdeth fast his integrity, although thou movedst
> Me against him, to destroy him without cause."
> And the Satan answered the Lord, and said, "Skin 2:4
> for skin, yea, all that a man hath will he give for
> his life. But put forth Thine hand now, and touch 2:5
> his bone and his flesh, and he will curse Thee to
> Thy face." And the Lord said unto the Satan, "Be- 2:6
> hold, he is in thine hand; but save his life."

Most commentators today think that Job's affliction was elephantiasis. Though I do not agree with them, I have relegated diagnosis to an appendix, for those who care. We are not concerned with pathology. As Job is an individual who represents Everyman; so his affliction is a particular disease that represents every sorrow.

It is not clear whether Job was out upon the ashes, bewailing his tragic loss, when the sickness came, or whether he went there afterward. Outside an Arabian town even today is an ash-heap for burned animal dung. This would make an ideal place to acquire infection. Some have inferred that Job was cast there, beyond the city, as a leper; for such was the crude isolation technique in other days. But the Old Testament conjunction of sorrow and ashes should provide sufficient reason for his choice of a mourning-place. To us it seems odd; in another age it seemed natural that one who knew intense grief should resort to the place of stench and filth to grieve.

Likewise it is not clear whether Job's wife spoke in scorn or in love. If in scorn, she meant that God had found out Job's secret sin, and was punishing him. But if she spoke in love, Job's wife suggests that since life is hopeless, he should give it up quickly. It was widely believed that a blasphemer would be smitten with instant death. Love could understandably urge one to turn from pain to oblivion. Whatever her motive in speaking, the advice constituted Job's most cruel burden of grief. As the plot develops, it becomes increasingly clear that the heaviest sorrow of all is

Job's alienation from God. Though he never alludes directly
to his wife's admonition, it remains a burning possibility
that he will yield to it, and die. When he most needs her
spiritual support, Job finds that his wife has withdrawn it.
Hence Augustine called her "the adjutant of the devil."
Whether her motive was good or bad, the advice she gave
was evil.

Job's response is more courteous in Hebrew than in English.
He rejects the advice forthwith, but not in quite so caustic
a manner as the English would indicate. Foolishness, with
us, denotes intellectual weakness. Among the Hebrews the
term denoted a failure to perceive spiritual values. In any
case, Job does not call his wife a fool, but tells her that she
is using foolish language. Since Job's children had lived
in close affection, one must presume that there had been
close affection between the parents. Love and grief could
lead a woman to utter horrible advice to her husband. Job
understands that his wife is beside herself in sorrow, and he
responds courteously.

The Satan had claimed confidently that Job would sin
with his lips. Instead Job praises God when his wife, all unknowing, urges him to fulfill the Satan's prophecy by blas-
pheming. He does not recognize that the Satan has any part
in his sorrows. And if he had recognized it, how much difference would that have made? Faith knows that there are
many purposes, not God's, at work in the world. Faith claims,
though, that all these ultimately serve the purpose of God.

> So went the Satan forth from the presence of the   2:7
> Lord, and smote Job with sore boils from the sole
> of his foot unto his crown. And he took him a   2:8
> potsherd to scrape himself withal; and he sat down
> among the ashes. Then said his wife unto him,   2:9
> "Dost thou still retain thine integrity? Curse God,
> and die." But he said unto her, "Thou speakest   2:10
> as one of the foolish women speaketh. What! shall
> we receive good at the hand of God, and shall we
> not receive evil?" In all this did not Job sin with
> his lips.

Job's three comforters, and the fourth who is introduced later, are among the most reviled men in the entire Bible. Yet those who so readily criticize them are making the comforters' favorite mistake. They are ignoring the evidence. The evidence, spread throughout the Book of Job, shows us men of faith, love, and vigorous intellect, who have tackled a task too big for them. He who would be a counsellor under any circumstances has a difficult time of it. He who counsels with one in utter despair is blessed indeed if he does not increase the despair. Every pastor recognizes that he too has committed the comforters' errors. Few are in any position to throw stones at the four who came to help Job. Our purpose is not to condemn or to praise, but to understand. In the Book of Job we find four well-intentioned, thoughtful men who speak too soon, say too much, and say the wrong things.

In the vocabulary of counselling today, the prime sin is rejection, and the prime necessity acceptance. A good counsellor accepts the other *person,* especially when in disagreement about some of his thoughts or actions. Job's comforters, on the contrary, grow so angry with him that they threaten, abuse, contradict, insult and argue with a man in desperate pain. It is difficult not to make these mistakes.

There is no discernible symbolism in the three comforters' names: Eliphaz, Bildad, and Zophar. (Elihu means "My God is He.") Like most names in Hebrew, these probably once signified something, but the scholars are not agreed about the meanings today. If ever there was some symbolic significance, we have lost it. The lands from which the comforters came are likewise the subject of much learned dispute. If the dispute is ever settled, it will make no difference at all to the blessing God mediates through the Book of Job.

> Now when Job's three friends heard of all this evil 2:11
> that was come upon him, they came every one from
> his own place; Eliphaz the Temanite, and Bildad
> the Shuhite, and Zophar the Naamathite: for they
> had made an appointment together to come to
> mourn with him and to comfort him. And when 2:12
> they lifted up their eyes afar off, and knew him not,
> they lifted up their voice, and wept; and they rent

> every one his mantle, and sprinkled dust upon
> their heads toward heaven. So they sat down with   2:13
> him upon the ground seven days and seven nights,
> and none spake a word unto him: for they saw
> that his grief was very great.

Drawn by ties of friendship and faith, the comforters
came to help Job in his desolate need. Let him who has
always been successful in helping others criticize if he will.
Certainly Job is harsh with his friends. Let him who has
never known pain criticize Job for that; the rest of us can
understand. But from his depth of harshness, Job cries out
for human compassion:

> Have pity upon me, have pity upon me,   19:21
>   O ye my friends;
> for the hand of God hath touched me.

Even while rejecting his friends, he yearns for their friendship.

When first the comforters saw Job they could not even recognize him, so disfigured was his face. They expressed their
sympathy with extravagant oriental gestures, tearing their
mantles, and casting dust upon their heads. For seven days
and seven nights they joined with Job in compassionate
silence. During this period, Job fell from his former sub-
missive faith into a mood of despair that is almost total.

II. JOB'S LAMENT 3:1-26

A. The curse upon life 3:1-10

B. Why died I not? 3:11-19

C. The longing for death 3:20-26

Job's Lament 3:1—26

> After this opened Job his mouth,   3:1
>   and cursed his day.

Job has been brooding in silent misery over the tragedies that have befallen him. He cannot turn for strength to his children — they are dead. He cannot turn to his wife — she has urged him to curse God and die. Even God seems not to care. Job knows that he is in desperate danger of losing the last shreds of his faith. When the comforters come, Job believes that at last he is with someone who will understand. They have mourned with him in mute sorrow. Now, Job mistakenly thinks, he can speak his thoughts in full confidence that his friends will sympathize. Not least among Job's sorrows is the burden the comforters add by withholding their sympathy. In the chapter before us, Job thinks that he is speaking to a compassionate audience. In later chapters, he recognizes that he is arguing down hostile critics. Here, he still believes himself among friends.

You will note in the lament a pattern that is repeated in almost every following speech of Job's, until he hears the Voice from the Whirlwind. He begins speaking in despair. As he speaks there comes a flash of the divine. For a moment God's light shines through the clouds. Then the darkness closes in, and the section ends in despair.

> Let the day perish wherein I was born,   3:3
>   and the night in which it was said,
>   "There is a man child conceived."
> Let that day be darkness;   3:4
>   let not God regard it from above,
>   neither let the light shine upon it.
> Let darkness and the shadow of death stain it;   3:5
>   let a cloud dwell upon it;
>   let the blackness of the day terrify it.

> As for that night, let darkness seize upon it;   3:6
>   let it not be joined unto the days of the year;
>   let it not come into the number of the months.
> Lo, let that night be solitary;   3:7
>   let no joyful voice come therein.
> Let them curse it that curse the day,   3:8
>   who are ready to raise up their mourning.
> Let the stars of the twilight thereof be dark;   3:9
>   let it look for light, but have none;
>   neither let it see the dawning of the day:
> Because it shut not up the doors of my   3:10
>   mother's womb,
>   nor hid sorrow from mine eyes.

The curse is a powerful expression of despair, in which Job begs that the night of his conception and the day of his birth be blotted from the calendar. Apparently the ancient Hebrews thought that a day or night had a semi-independent existence of its own. (Cf Psalm 19:2.) A day would recur, year after year. So, in theory at least, a day could be destroyed. But there is no need to examine calendrical beliefs here. Job is expressing his feelings, not astrophysics. He is cursing his very existence. Insofar as a curse has any factual meaning, Job means: If that day had not been, then I would not be.

Yet, in the midst of his anguish, Job calls upon God:

> Let that day be darkness;   3:4
>   let not God regard it from above.

Perhaps this mention of God is the mere result of religious habit. It is scarce worth dignifying as a gleam of light in abysmal darkness. In his black cursing, Job calls upon God to curse. Still, one must note that Job does call upon God.

Job reinforces the curse with a question. It is a characteristic of Hebrew poetry that this question is asked four times, with slight variations. As you read through Job, you will notice many instances of this same poetic device, technically known as parallelism, in which the poet reinforces a mood by just such repetition. Parallelism is the outstanding formal characteristic of Hebrew poetry. One speaks hesitantly about the formal characteristics of poetry today, though until recently a poem in English was expressed in metre, and frequently in rhyme. C. S. Lewis, in the work previously mentioned, says of parallelism, "It is (according to one's point of view) either a wonderful piece of luck or a wise provision of God's, that poetry which was to be turned into all languages should have as its chief formal characteristic one that does not disappear (as mere metre does) in translation" (*Reflections on the Psalms,* page 4).

Each of the four questions is implicit in the first. Job asks, Since I was conceived and born, why did I survive? The reference to the knees refers to a Hebrew custom. A newborn child was placed upon the father's knee, as a mark that the father received the child as his own.

Why died I not from the womb?	3:11
why did I not perish at birth?	
Why did the knees receive me?	3:12
or why the breasts that I should suck?	

There follows a song of matchless beauty about the sleep of death. This song, and several following passages that concern death, trouble many Christians; for Job here states flatly that there is no meaningful life following physical death.

The Bible is a progressive revelation. Many seed-concepts grow and develop in the Old Testament, but do not really bear fruit until one comes to the New. As far as we can discover, at no time did the Hebrews ever think (officially) about death as total extinction. Instead they believed that when the body died, the soul went to Sheol, a dim sort of half-conscious existence devoid alike of glory and of pain. (See Psalm 6:5; Psalm 39:13; Psalm 88:4-12; Ecclesiastes 9:10.) A modern materialist would say that Sheol is a form of belief in immortality. But a Christian can recognize in this shadowy concept only the seed of his belief in eternal life. The seed-truth expressed by the Sheol-concept is that the soul is more than a mere function of the physical organism.

In the Providence of God, the Book of Job was one important means of showing the way from Sheol to the New Jerusalem, though one would never guess this by reading chapter 3 in isolation from the rest of the Book. Here, and in following passages, Job thinks deeply upon the idea of life after death, and bitterly he concludes that there is only the darkness of Sheol. The commentators disagree vigorously about 19:25-27, but many find that passage a firm statement of life, real life, after bodily death. Whether they are correct or not, I believe still that the Book of Job forces the reader to recognize at least that there is a profound inconsistency between the idea of death as virtual extinction and the idea that God is love. This thought will be examined more carefully in the proper place, 14:7-15. In the meantime, we shall follow the leading of the Holy Spirit along the tortuous way of Job's pilgrimage. When Job, despairing, denies the possibility of eternal life, we shall recognize that this is the voice of human grief, not God's final word on the subject.

The Christian reader will say that several Old Testament passages point to life after death. The ones usually cited are: Psalms 17:15; 23:4, 6; 49:15; 73:24; 139:8; Isaiah 26:19; and Daniel 12:2, 3. To these I would add Job 19:25-27 and 26:6. Even without these "proof texts" (one of which is much disputed) the basic argument running through the Book of Job leads indirectly but logically to the conclusion, "I am the Resurrection and the Life" (John 11:25.)

By New Testament time, many Hebrews believed that physical death is not the end, as instanced by Jesus' elliptical statement, "If it were not so I would have told you" (John 14:2b.) But the Sadducees, who were the biblical literalists of the time, denied this belief. They stated, correctly, that it cannot be proved from the Pentateuch, hence they rejected it.

What did Job believe about death and immortality before his tragedy? I do not know. The Book we are examining shows that he had a flash of insight into the truth, as recorded in chapters 19 and 26. However, at the moment we are considering chapter 3, where Job examines the idea of life after death and finds only a shadowy semi-existence, for which he yearns. There kings and princes are one with the unborn infants, the weary, the prisoners and the slaves. All are at rest. I have known Christians, in moments of physical pain, to make statements that would be unthinkable under other circumstances. Job is a desperate man. His statements

about death should be read in the light of that fact, with
the knowledge that God raised him from despair and lifted
him into the light.

> For now should I have lain still and been quiet,   3:13
>   I should have slept:
>   then had I been at rest
> With kings and counsellors of the earth,   3:14
>   which built desolate places for themselves;
> Or with princes that had gold,   3:15
>   who filled their houses with silver:
> Or as an hidden untimely birth I had not been;   3:16
>   as infants which never saw light.
> There the wicked cease from troubling;   3:17
>   and there the weary be at rest.
> There the prisoners rest together;   3:18
>   they hear not the voice of the oppressor.
> The small and great are there;   3:19
>   and the servant is free from his master.

After singing the beauty of death, Job poignantly expresses
his longing to die.

> Wherefore is light given to him that is in misery, 3:20
>   and life unto the bitter in soul;
> Which long for death, but it cometh not;   3:21
>   and dig for it more than for hid treasures;
> Which rejoice exceedingly, and are glad,   3:22
>   when they can find the grave?
> Why is light given to a man whose way is hid,   3:23
>   and whom God hath hedged in?
> For my sighing cometh before I eat,   3:24
>   and my roarings are poured out like the waters.
> For the thing which I greatly feared is come   3:25
>   upon me,
>   and that which I was afraid of is come unto me,
> I was not in safety, neither had I rest,   3:26
>   neither was I quiet; yet trouble came.

Again Job questions, Why? Why is light given to a man
whom God has hedged in? And again, in the uttermost depth
of grief, Job expresses the faintest sign of hope; for he rec-

ognizes that his sorrows, somehow, come from God. He longs to be free from his sorrows. He longs to be free from the burden of life. His longing for God is not yet articulate.

Never has human despair been depicted with deeper insight and greater power. Job's is not the diseased melancholy of a sick mind or a warped personality. It is the response of an essentially healthy, vigorous, searching mind to the inescapable fact of pain.

To the religious skeptic there is no problem of pain. Random chance, operating within the blind laws of statistical probability, brought us into being. Whether we suffer or rejoice is indifferent to the blind mechanism of chance. Only the sufferer or the rejoicer cares. But to faith, pain presents one of the supreme problems. Does God care? Then why does He permit this? Job has posed the problem of pain better than anyone else, before or since, in the pathetic confidence that his comforters will answer the question.

Almost all of us have known moments, at least, of Job-like despair. The gloomy satirist, Jonathan Swift, used to read Job 3 each year at the time of his birthday. Many of my friends, in time of deep sorrow, have found great spiritual consolation in Job's bitter words. It helps those in the valley of the shadow to know that others have passed this way before, and come into the light on the other side.

Mary Ellen Chase, in *The Bible and the Common Reader*, listing the most beautiful parts of Job, names first of all chapter 3. (The others mentioned are chapters 28, 29, 38, and 39.) Even within the Book of Job, the heights of beauty in the third chapter are seldom equaled and never surpassed.

The First Cycle of Speeches 4:1—14:22

The comforters' argument sounds hollow and almost meaningless, when one encounters it in the Book of Job. Take the words out and examine them apart from Job's anguish. Then they sound solid and reassuring. That is the trouble with the argument. It is a comfortable theory about divine Providence carefully insulated from the facts. Such Pollyanna credulity often passes for faith in the twentieth century. But faith demands that one examine the facts of the situation. The comforters' theory is that, despite occasional variations from the norm, the innocent are vindicated and the wicked are punished. What they fail to mention is that the vindication or punishment may take centuries to work out. But Job's pain is in the here and now. He points out scornfully:

> Ye say, "God layeth up iniquity for his children!"   21:19
>   Let Him reward the wicked himself,
>   that he may know it.
> Let his own eyes see his destruction,   21:20
>   and let him drink of the wrath of the Almighty.
> For what pleasure hath he in his house after him?   21:21

One likes to think of an argument as a train of thought that begins somewhere, and goes somewhere, and gets somewhere. But one can find almost no progression of thought among the comforters. Job progresses. They stand still, upon the ideas so capably expressed in Eliphaz' first speech. If we examine this first speech in considerable detail, it will not be necessary to examine all that follow with the same care.

FIRST SPEECH OF ELIPHAZ 4:1—5:27

When Job has spoken, Eliphaz, presumably the eldest comforter, begs leave to respond:

> If we assay to commune with thee,   4:2
> wilt thou be grieved?
> but who can withhold himself from speaking?

Eliphaz has made his first mistake. It is sometimes quite difficult to keep from rushing in with words of consolation that further batter and bruise a wounded soul. After a week's silence, it would require almost super-human restraint to keep from speaking. So, although he has little of value to offer, Eliphaz speaks. At least his words begin on a courteous level. Take them to your heart. These are the last civil words you will encounter for many long chapters.

> Behold, thou hast instructed many,   4:3
> and thou hast strengthened the weak hands.
> Thy words have upholden him that was falling,   4:4
> and thou hast strengthened the feeble knees.
> But now it is come upon thee, and thou faintest;   4:5
> it toucheth thee, and thou art troubled.

In chapters 29-31, you can discover how admirably Eliphaz has described Job's helpfulness in the days of his strength. Is there now perhaps a touch of scorn in his voice? "He saved others, himself he cannot save" (Mark 15:31.)

After the exquisite courtesy of his request, Eliphaz sets the stage for all the following discussion:

> Is not thy fear of God thy confidence?   4:6
> and thy hope the integrity of thy ways?

Unconsciously Eliphaz has touched the root of Job's difficulty. The comforters and Job alike stress, not divine love, but man's striving after God; not divine sovereignty, but man's integrity. And here is the weakness in their position. Though they talk learnedly enough about God, their faith is essentially man-centered. Job does not really find himself until he is lost in God.

Eliphaz now presents his comfortable theory. Before one has finished reading the Book of Job, these thoughts will sound tinny and mocking. Yet one hears the same thoughts echoing over radio pulpits in our day. Has the passage of centuries improved an idea that was false to begin with?

> Remember, I pray thee, who ever perished,   4:7
>> being innocent?
> or where were the righteous cut off?
> Even as I have seen, they that plow iniquity,   4:8
>> and sow wickedness, reap the same.
> By the blast of God they perish,   4:9
>> and by the breath of His nostrils
>> are they consumed.

In words of breathtaking power, Eliphaz describes a mystic experience of God's awful holiness. Divine mystery and glory have overpowered and overwhelmed him. In the voluminous literature of mysticism, Eliphaz' brief description has never been surpassed. He describes vividly the awe, akin to terror, that man feels when God is nigh. A gust of wind signified the divine presence. Eliphaz' awe deepened as he strained his eyes to behold a form that was not a form. Before him was an image upon which his eyes could not focus. And to his ears there came a voice.

> Now a thing was secretly brought to me,   4:12
>> and mine ear received a little thereof.
> In thoughts from the visions of the night,   4:13
>> when deep sleep falleth on men,
> Fear came upon me, and trembling,   4:14
>> which made all my bones to shake.
> Then a spirit passed before my face;   4:15
>> the hair of my flesh stood up:
> It stood still, but I could not discern   4:16
>> the form thereof:
> an image was before mine eyes;
> there was silence, and I heard a voice.

After the unspeakable grandeur of Eliphaz' description, the message received comes with a disappointing shock. (Readers of mystical literature have encountered a similar shock on other occasions.) From his overpowering experience, Eliphaz has extracted nothing to strengthen Job. He reports the immeasurable otherness that is God. "Transcendence" is the theological term. But Job never questions that God is transcendent. Job's question concerns divine love. Does God care? If He cares, then why is this happening? Eliphaz answers the inescapable question of faith by hinting that Job deserves his calamity. Can mortal man be righteous before God?

In Eliphaz' discourse is a tragic mixture of truth and falsehood. Almost every profound religious experience entails the sense of divine transcendence together with that of human limitation. (See Isaiah 6:1-8, for example.) But to Eliphaz, man's finiteness is equal to moral guilt in itself. And, far worse, he seems to be saying that divine power is basically amoral. (This conclusion, too, is frequent among the mystics.) He depicts God as being so exalted that He does not really care about those who dwell in houses of clay. He crushes them as carelessly as a man crushes a moth.

No one could question the accuracy with which Eliphaz describes the human plight. We dwell in houses of clay with foundations in the dust. Man is crushed and destroyed from morning to evening. People perish, and many of them without wisdom. Should we therefore conclude that God does not care?

> "Shall mortal man be more just than God?   4:17
>   shall a man be more pure than his Maker?"
> Behold, He put no trust in his servants;   4:18
>   and His angels He charged with folly:
> How much less in them that dwell in houses of clay, 4:19
>   whose foundation is in the dust,
>   which are crushed before the moth?
> They are destroyed from morning to evening: 4:20
>   they perish forever without any regarding it.
> Doth not their excellency which is in them go away? 4:21
>   they die, even without wisdom.

The following verse is cryptic, to say the least. Probably Eliphaz is warning Job against an appeal to angelic intercession. Thus early in the poem is suggested the developing thought that leads to the cry for the "Arbiter" (9:33), the "Witness" (16:19), and finally the "Redeemer" (19:25.) Or possibly Eliphaz is but warning Job that an appeal to human experience will confirm his words.

> Call now, if there be any that will answer thee;   5:1
>   and to which of the holy ones wilt thou turn?

Eliphaz swings with true zest into the path that the comforters tread with such annoying confidence. The wicked prosper, but only for a short time.

For wrath killeth the foolish man,	5:2
and envy slayeth the silly one.	
I have seen the foolish taking root:	5:3
but suddenly I cursed his habitation.	
His children are far from safety,	5:4
and they are crushed in the gate,	
neither is there any to deliver them.	
Whose harvest the hungry eateth up,	5:5
and taketh it even out of the thorns,	
and the robber swalloweth up their substance.	

Whether the ensuing thought is profound or silly depends upon the intent with which it is uttered. It is true that man must live in the environment of trouble, as inescapable as any other fact in nature. It is profoundly true that human sorrow develops — in most instances — from human sin. Indeed, one possible translation reads, "man begets sorrow." Moffatt translates, "man brings trouble on himself." As we have noticed, "man" is a term that can mean either "a particular individual" or "the human race." Eliphaz calmly ignores the distinction. What is true of man in the collective sense may or may not be true of man in the individual sense. Our nation, for example, has twice been dragged into an European war that had its origin when Charlemagne's sons could not agree upon a division of the empire. Indubitably, the sorrows we received from Wilhelm II and Adolph Hitler were caused by "man," but you and I did not originate them. So Eliphaz says something true in a context suggesting that Job, as an individual, is directly responsible for the sorrows that have come into his life. If this is his meaning, then his words are false.

Although affliction cometh not forth of the dust,	5:6
neither doth trouble spring out of the ground;	
Yet man is born unto trouble,	5:7
as the sparks fly upward.	

Eliphaz has forgotten about God's transcendent indifference to mortal pain. He advises Job to seek unto God and commit his cause to Him. What painful superiority lies in the advice: "If I were you . . ." It is easy to point out the blessings of the righteous, when one is himself blessed. It is easy to point out the affliction of the wicked, when someone else is afflicted. And with cool competence, Eliphaz points out both.

Eliphaz is leading up to a quotation, Proverbs 3:11a. The proverb is a generalization. Like most valid generalizations, it is true most of the time. But there are times in life when it is tactless or even false to stress a particular truth. It is true that sorrow has an intimate, inescapable connection with evil. But not all sorrow has. It is true that pain can have a therapeutic value. But not all pain has. (I was called from the typewriter to go to the hospital. A friend had just been critically injured in an accident. Half-crazed with pain and shock, he cried, "I've tried to be good. Why did this happen to me?" With Eliphaz looming before me, I decided that this was not the proper time to quote Proverbs 3:11.)

I would seek unto God,	5:8
and unto God would I commit my cause:	
Which doeth great things and unsearchable;	5:9
marvellous things without number:	
Who giveth rain upon the earth,	5:10
and sendeth waters upon the fields:	
To set up on high those that be low;	5:11
that those which mourn may be exalted to safety.	
He disappointeth the devices of the crafty,	5:12
so that their hands cannot perform	
their enterprise.	
He taketh the wise in their own craftiness;	5:13
and the counsel of the froward is carried headlong.	
They meet with darkness in the day-time,	5:14
and grope in the noon-day as in the night.	
But He saveth the poor from the sword,	5:15
from their mouth,	
and from the hand of the mighty.	
So the poor hath hope,	5:16
and iniquity stoppeth her mouth.	

> Behold, happy is the man whom God correcteth;   5:17
> therefore despise not thou the chastening
> of the Almighty.

Suppose Job does commit his cause to God. Suppose he learns to rejoice in his afflictions. What then? Then, Eliphaz promises, Job's illness will be cured, his flocks and herds will be restored, he will again know peace and prosperity. Once more children will play around his feet. Eliphaz' concluding words are insufferably smug. They fall with a leaden thud, after 5:26, which is the perfect poetic expression for the death of a godly, aged man.

> For He maketh sore, and bindeth up;   5:18
> He woundeth, and His hands make whole.
> He shall deliver thee in six troubles;   5:19
> yea, in seven there shall no evil touch thee.
> In famine He shall redeem thee from death;   5:20
> and in war from the power of the sword.
> Thou shalt be hid from the scourge of the tongue;   5:21
> neither shalt thou be afraid of destruction
> when it cometh.
> At destruction and famine thou shalt laugh;   5:22
> neither shalt thou be afraid of the beasts
> of the earth.
> For thou shalt be in league with the stones   5:23
> of the field;
> and the beasts of the field shall be at peace
> with thee.
> And thou shalt know that thy tabernacle   5:24
> shall be in peace;
> and thou shalt visit thy habitation,
> and shalt not sin.
> Thou shalt know also that thy seed shall be great,   5:25
> and thine offspring as the grass of the earth.
> Thou shalt come to thy grave in a full age,   5:26
> like as a shock of corn cometh in in its season.
> Lo this, we have searched it, so it is;   5:27
> hear it, and know thou it for thy good.

Eliphaz is demonstrably a man of keen intellect. He has marshalled his arguments and presented them with logic and vigor. He believes in God, and urges Job to commit his cause to Him. But there is, lurking within the logic, a touch of commercialism. Commit your cause to God, Job, and your flocks and herds will prosper once more. Is this the reason for devotion? Does man worship in order to have peace of mind, freedom from inhibitions, and success? This was the Satan's argument in the prologue. Eliphaz unknowingly agrees with the Satan.

Despite the brilliance of his logic, Eliphaz has failed completely to project his love to Job. That such love exists we can be very sure. Why else would one sit on an ash-heap with a friend, if not to express love? Can it be that there is a deep reason for Eliphaz' failure? Is his trouble, perhaps, that he does not really love God?

In the following speeches by the comforters, you will encounter the same propositions again and again. The principle arguments, in Eliphaz' order of presentation, are:

1. The righteous are blessed.
2. God is transcendent.
3. Man is unworthy of divine love.
4. Sorrow is closely connected with sin.
5. Evil is punished.
6. Suffering has a disciplinary value.
7. God will receive the one who turns to Him in faith.

No Christian could dispute any of these statements. Indeed, John Calvin says of the comforters' basic arguments:

> There is nothing in their propositions that we ought not to receive as if the Holy Spirit had pronounced it; for it is pure truth, these are the foundations of religion.
>
> —*Sermons from Job,* page 5.

The propositions that the comforters advance are sound theism. The use to which they are put frequently is unsound. The Joban poet certainly accepted the propositions, but he rejected most vigorously the practice of treating faith as a set of disconnected pious answers to be applied unthinkingly to human problems. Job's comforters are so completely exasperating because of their smug assurance that they understand the whole truth, when in fact they know but the aspects of the truth. The blind men examining the elephant reported their findings correctly. Their error lay in denying that some one else might also be reporting correctly. So the comforters make many true statements about divine Providence. But they deny that the righteous suffer. We who see the Cross as the power of God unto salvation can never join them in this denial.

A few words in defense of Job's comforters are in order. The Joban poet has dealt harshly enough with them. They were pompous, opinionated, blind, and a lot of other bad things. But they did *not* say:

1. "Buck up, Job old man, things might be worse."
They did *not* say:

2. "It's all in your mind, Job. Think positively."
They did *not* say:

3. "I don't believe God had anything to do with this."
Since at least one of these three remarks is offered to practically everyone who mourns in our country today, I believe that Job's comforters should be given great credit for refraining from any or all of them.

JOB'S FIRST RESPONSE TO ELIPHAZ 6:1—7:21

When Eliphaz has finished, Job responds, justifying his right to complain. He openly accuses God, comparing Him with a hunter who uses poisoned arrows, whose hounds are closing in on the wounded and dying beast.

> Oh that my grief were thoroughly weighed, 6:2
>   and my calamity laid in the balances together!
> For now it would be heavier than the sand of the sea: 6:3
>   therefore my words are swallowed up.
> For the arrows of the Almighty are within me, 6:4
>   the poison whereof drinketh up my spirit:
>   the terrors of God do set themselves in array
>   against me.

To the friend who has offered so little consolation, Job makes an invidious contrast, suggesting that Eliphaz' own ease and prosperity have made him incapable of true sympathy with one who suffers. This contrast is unfair, but still in daily use.

> Doth the wild ass bray when he hath grass? 6:5
>   or loweth the ox over his fodder?

Life has become flat and tasteless. (Modern translators, in
their laudable zeal for accuracy, have taken a long step backward with the following verse. The white of an egg is, to
most, the epitome of nothingness. For this, the Jewish Version substitutes "the juice of mallows" and the Revised Standard Version "the slime of purslane." Neither expression says
anything to the modern reader. Which is more important,
to translate out of Hebrew or to translate into English?) The
dreariness and pain that a normal, healthy person shuns are
Job's constant diet, his "sorrowful meat."

> Can that which is unsavory be eaten without salt?   6:6
>   or is there any taste in the white of an egg?
> The things that my soul refused to touch   6:7
>   are as my sorrowful meat.

Job voices again his hope for death, saying that he would
exult even in the pain of dying, with the knowledge that
his conscience is clear.

> Oh that I might have my request;   6:8
>   and that God would grant me the thing
>   that I long for!
> Even that it would please God to destroy me;   6:9
>   that He would let loose His hand,
>   and cut me off!
> Then should I yet have comfort;   6:10
>   yea, I would harden myself in sorrow:
>   let Him not spare;
>   for I have not concealed the words
>   of the Holy One.

Eliphaz has urged Job to be patient and to hope; but he
can endure his anguish no longer. He cries that there are
limits to human strength, as he examines fleetingly the man-
centered faith Eliphaz has urged him to adopt, finding that
there is no resource, physical or spiritual, in it. Quite the
contrary, Eliphaz' advice has driven the wisdom out of Job.
(The Authorized Version treats 6:13 as a question. The
interpretation remains in either case.)

> What is my strength, that I should hope?   6:11
>   and what is mine end, that I should prolong
>   my life?

> Is my strength the strength of stones?   6:12
>   or is my flesh of brass?
> My help is not in me   6:13
>   and my wisdom is driven from me.

There follows a complex verse. All translators have had grave difficulty with it; for it can yield one of several meanings, each with theological problems of its own. The most probable reading, to my mind, is:

> He who withholdeth kindness from a friend   6:14
>   forsaketh the fear of the Almighty.

If one accept this translation, then the verse means that faith is expressed in terms of kindness, and conversely, one who is unkind denies his faith. Is it right that a man in anguish should receive reproaches from a friend?

Job continues, comparing his disappointment in Eliphaz with that of desert travelers who approach a brook, expecting to quench their thirst, but when they arrive, the brook has dried under the scorching sun.

> My brethren have dealt deceitfully as a brook,   6:15
>   and as the stream of brooks they pass away;
> Which are blackish by reason of the ice,   6:16
>   and wherein the snow is hid:
> What time they wax warm, they vanish: 6:17
>   when it is hot, they are consumed out of
>   their place.
> The paths of their way are turned aside;   6:18
>   they go to nothing, and perish.
> The caravans of Tema looked,   6:19
>   the companies of Sheba waited expectantly.
> They were confounded because they had hoped;   6:20
>   they came thither, and were disappointed.
> For such have ye become unto me,   6:21
>   ye see my casting down, and are afraid.

Job has barbed his disappointment with a keen psychological thrust. These who came to comfort are themselves terrified by Job's affliction. Is there here perhaps a suggestion that they fear the stigma of guilt by association?

With a snarl, Job points out forcibly that he has asked
no material gift, nothing but sympathy. And he has received
only censure. But censure for what?

Did I say, "Bring unto me?"   6:22
   or, "Give a reward for me of your substance?"
Or, "Deliver me from the enemy's hand?"   6:23
   or, "Redeem me from the hand of the mighty?"
Teach me, and I will hold my tongue;   6:24
   and cause me to understand wherein I have erred.

Again Job complains of the weariness of life. The nights
are endless torment, yet life passes with incredible speed. Job
compares himself, and all of suffering humanity, with the
exhausted slave for whom life holds no more than a shadow
in which he can rest, or the hireling whose wages will but
sustain physical existence. There is no hope.

As a servant earnestly desireth the shadow,   7:2
   and as a hireling looketh for the reward
     of his work:
So am I made to possess months of vanity,   7:3
   and wearisome nights are appointed to me.
When I lie down, I say,   7:4
  "When shall I arise, and the night be gone?"
   and I am full of tossings to and fro
     unto the dawning of the day.
My flesh is clothed with worms and clods of dust;   7:5
   my skin is broken, and become loathsome.
My days are swifter than a weaver's shuttle,   7:6
   and are spent without hope.

Turning away from Eliphaz, Job speaks to God. Surely
the prayer that follows is the most amazing in the entire
Scripture, if not in all devotional literature. It begins on a
plaintive note, rises to a bellow of sheer rage, then dies away
in a whimper.

First the plaintive note: Once more Job examines the
possibility of life after death, and foresees only the darkness of Sheol. Since earthly life represents Job's last opportunity to speak with God, Job will speak.

O remember that my life is wind: 7:7
   mine eye shall no more see good.

> The eye of him that hath seen me shall see   7:8
>   me no more:
> Thine eyes are upon me, and I am not.
> As the cloud is consumed and vanisheth away;   7:9
>   so he that goeth down to Sheol shall
>   come up no more.
> He shall return no more to his house,   7:10
>   neither shall his place know him any more.
> Therefore I will not refrain my mouth;   7:11
>   I will speak in the anguish of my spirit;
>   I will complain in the bitterness of my soul.

Then the bellow of rage: Job snarls a bitter reproach to God. "Am I a sea or a whale?" This is one of several symbolic references to the sea and the great sea-monster Tiamat of Babylonian mythology. These were subdued and chained by the Creator, lest they break forth and destroy the world. Job asks, Am I as dangerous as all that? Fearful dreams haunt Job's wakeful nights, so that he longs for death, and screams at God, "Let me alone."

> Am I a sea, or a whale,   7:12
>   that Thou settest a watch over me?
> When I say, "My bed shall comfort me,   7:13
>   my couch shall ease my complaint,"
> Then Thou scarest me with dreams,   7:14
>   and terrifiest me through visions;
> So that my soul chooseth strangling,   7:15
>   and death rather than my life.
> I loathe it; I would not live alway: 7:16
>   let me alone; for my days are vanity.

The bellow of rage continues as Job burlesques the words of Psalm 8:5:

> What is man, that Thou shouldest magnify him?   7:17
>   and that Thou shouldest set Thine heart
>   upon him?
> And that Thou shouldest visit him every morning,   7:18
>   and try him every moment?
> How long wilt Thou not depart from me,   7:19
>   nor let me alone till I swallow down my spittle?

Note how the mood shifts to a whimper of pain. Suppose, for sake of the argument, I have sinned, have I harmed God enough to deserve this?

> If I have sinned, what do I unto Thee,   7:20
>   O Thou Preserver of men?
> Why hast Thou set me as a mark against Thee,
>   so that I am a burden unto Thee?

There is a debatable question: Does Job speak of the burden upon himself (as in the Authorized Version) or upon God? Most commentators today believe that he speaks of himself as a burden to God. Here in the pit is a flash of light. For a moment Job realizes that God cares when a man suffers. Though the poison of God's arrows is in Job's flesh, God, as well as Job, is burdened. Job has looked about him in the pit, and found there the full horror of the shade, but he is discovering that God too is in the pit, looking for Job.

Perhaps you recall the time when you were a child and your parents did something that you thought most unjust. You went away and sulked. Thoughts of death filled your mind. You pictured yourself in your casket, and then your parents were truly sorry. You did not realize it at the time, but indirectly you were assuring yourself that they really loved you, despite their failure to be ideal parents. If today you are a parent, you realize that one's perspective changes in regard to these matters. Today perhaps your child is thinking such thoughts about you. But you know what your child longs to believe, that your action, so distasteful to the child, was undertaken in love. So Job in fancy reverts to a childish death-dream. Still rebellious and unconvinced, he gives indirect testimony to the belief that God is love.

> And why dost Thou not pardon my transgression,   7:21
>   and take away mine iniquity?
> for now shall I sleep in the dust;
> and Thou shalt seek me in the morning,
>   but I shall not be.

FIRST SPEECH OF BILDAD   8:1-22

Bildad is shocked at Job's impetuous words. Doubtless he feels that Eliphaz has been sufficiently polite. At any rate, he plunges into a biting condemnation that, for sheer rudeness, would be difficult to excel. First he calls Job a windbag. Then he twists the knife in Job's wound by announcing that the children were killed as punishment for their sins. Bildad, like Eliphaz, has decided that if a fact does not mesh with his theory, he should ignore it. If a fact is missing, he will invent one. So, gratuitously, Bildad decrees that the dead children were all sinners, hence God had no choice but to destroy them. It is pressing the limits of friendship to tell a man in pain that he talks too much. As for adding another burden of grief in regard to the dead children, doubtless it was well intentioned.

How long wilt thou speak these things?	8:2
and how long shall the words of thy mouth be like a strong wind?	
Doth God pervert judgment,	8:3
or doth the Almighty pervert justice,	
If thy children have sinned against Him,	8:4
and He have cast them away for their transgression?	

Bildad's theology is simple and shallow. He clothes sordid thoughts in radiant garments. You have often heard this following idea, but have you ever heard it so well expressed?

If thou wouldest seek unto God betimes,	8:5
and make thy supplication to the Almighty:	
If thou wert pure and upright;	8:6
surely now He would awake for thee,	
and make the habitation of thy righteousness prosperous.	

This is, with a vengeance, the man-centered faith. Turn on the tap marked piety, and out will gush a stream of blessing. Man is the author of his own salvation. Moral life is the price he pays for prosperity. God will bestir Himself on your behalf if you just bestir yourself on His.

Even Bildad cannot deny that the wicked seem, sometimes, to prosper. Again, he invents a few facts to bolster his case. He decrees that the prosperity of the wicked is short-lived.

> He shall lean upon his house,   8:15
>   but it shall not stand:
>   he shall hold it fast, but it shall not endure.

The speech that began in such rude bitterness concludes in tones of genuine friendship. Bildad seems almost to regret his earlier violence, as he promises that all will be well, if Job will but follow his good advice.

> Behold, God will not cast away an innocent man,   8:20
>   neither will He help the evil doers;
> Till He fill thy mouth with laughing,   8:21
>   and thy lips with rejoicing.
> They that hate thee shall be clothed with shame;   8:22
>   and the dwelling place of the wicked shall
>   come to nought.

JOB'S FIRST RESPONSE TO BILDAD 9:1–10:22

In the ninth and tenth chapters, Job ostensibly is answering Bildad. But he refers far more often to the thoughts that Eliphaz has expressed. In this section Job accepts Eliphaz' points that God is all-powerful, that man cannot be just in God's sight, and that the finite cannot comprehend the infinite.

Man cannot understand God, neither can man hope to save himself. Unless God saves us, we are lost indeed. This is what one might call the bad news of the gospel. It runs directly contrary to the good opinion twentieth century man has of himself. The comforters are expressing this good opinion quite capably. (It is not so modern, after all.) Job is out exploring the realities of the human situation and discovering that man is lost. From this position of near-despair, he cries for an Arbiter who can intercede with God for man, and with man for God. In the valley of the shadow, Job discovers the need for Christ.

First of all, Job dismisses Bildad by contemptuously agreeing with all he has said. Then he reverts to Eliphaz' claim (4:17 f.) that God is just and man is not. "Just" is used here, as often in the Bible, to designate the innocent party in a lawsuit. More and more, from this point on, the idea of the lawsuit with God comes to dominate Job's thoughts.

It is difficult to tell, a good deal of the time, whether Job or God is the one on trial. Job likens himself to an honest but stupid witness whom an unscrupulous lawyer is tying into knots. Of course he cannot be just before God. He could not answer one question in a thousand.

I know it is so of a truth:	9:2
but how should man be just with God?	
If he will contend with Him,	9:3
he cannot answer Him one of a thousand.	

Job looks with awe at the power of God's work in nature, and admits that he cannot contend with God. Yet, admitting this, Job contends. Though with his lips he denies that God is just, Job continues to seek justice from God.

He is wise in heart, and mighty in strength;	9:4
who hath hardened himself against Him,	
and hath prospered?	
He who removeth the mountains, and they	9:5
know it not,	
when He overturneth them in His anger;	
Who shaketh the earth out of her place,	9:6
and the pillars thereof tremble;	
Who commandeth the sun, and it riseth not,	9:7
and sealeth up the stars.	
Who alone spreadeth out the heavens,	9:8
and treadeth upon the waves of the sea.	
Who doeth great things past finding out;	9:10
yea, and wonders without number.	

So much for the power of God. Job never calls this into question. But he seeks and cannot find God's moral purpose.

Trapped in a pain-filled world, without confidence that God is righteous, Job gives way to despair. We have marked several low points, and shall mark several more, but here in the ninth chapter is the lowest point in Job's spiritual pilgrimage. This is the closest he comes to accepting his wife's brutal admonition, "Curse God and die."

For He breaketh me with a tempest,	9:17
and multiplieth my wounds without cause.	

He will not suffer me to take my breath,   9:18
    but filleth me with bitterness.
If I speak of strength, lo, He is strong: 9:19
    and if of judgment, who shall set me a time
      to plead?
If I justify myself, mine own mouth shall   9:20
    condemn me:
    if I say, "I am upright," it shall also
      prove me perverse.
I am blameless: I regard not myself;   9:21
    I despise my life.
It is all one—therefore I say,   9:22
    "He destroyeth the upright and the wicked."
If the scourge slay suddenly,   9:23
    He will laugh at the trial of the innocent.
The earth is given into the hand of the wicked: 9:24
    He covereth the faces of the judges thereof;
    if it be not He, who then is it?

The thoughts form a serious problem of faith for many devout Christians. Here in the Holy Bible a righteous man speaks words that are blasphemous. It is one thing to say that the upright and the wicked both perish—that much we all have observed. Everyone who can read a newspaper knows that the wicked frequently prosper, and that justice is sometimes quite blind. Here Job is but reporting the facts, correctly. But when he says that God laughs at the trial of the innocent, he is getting away from sociology and into theology, and remarkably bad theology at that.

Why are such words in the Bible? *First,* I suggest that the Bible is a revelation of human nature as well as the divine Mystery. Job is acting the way human beings act in time of pain. We who believe that God is all-understanding must believe that He understands Job, and the countless million others who have stormed and raged against Him in their hour of agony. *Second,* Job is being honest with himself, his comforters, and with God. The comforters are committing a sin that is peculiar to the devout. They are tailoring the facts to fit their dogma. Job relentlessly exposes the facts. They would cramp truth to fit into their mold. Job seeks to express the truth. *Third,* the Book of Job is not ended on the note of denial. God accepts Job, who has blasphemed, and then accepts the comforters after Job's intercession. The comforters do not blaspheme. Their words about God are pious and decorous. Evidently piety and decorum are not enough. Not yet is Job ready to hear God speaking from the whirlwind, but at least he notices that there is a whirlwind. *Fourth,* it is misrepresenting the Bible, or any other book, to take a sentence out of its total context. "He will laugh at the trials of the innocent," out of context, is a flat denial of all that we believe. But put those words into the mouth of one who is covered with boils, bereft of his children, and tormented by his friends, yet still seeking the truth—then they become an intelligible part of a person's salvation.

There is one way to avoid religious doubts, and that is to avoid thinking. Job chose to think, while his comforters chose to echo platitudes—in magnificent poetry to be sure. And God chose Job.

Through a series of negations, Job is coming into a position where complacency is shattered, but the heart is open to receive God. Bitterly, but correctly, he exposes the impossibility of salvation by works. Probably he alludes now to Psalm 51:7b, "Wash me, and I shall be whiter than snow," where the psalmist calls upon God to cleanse. But Job, still defiant, shouts that when a man cleanses himself, then God pushes him into the muddy ditch. In crude words of rustic vigor Job expresses something the twentieth century has forgotten. Man, spiritually speaking, is in a ditch and cannot climb out.

> If I wash myself with snow water,   9:30
>   and make my hands never so clean;
> Yet shalt Thou plunge me in the ditch,   9:31
>   and mine own clothes shall abhor me.

Job, in the ditch, shakes his muddy hand at the leaden sky. He has agreed with Eliphaz that God is transcendent, beyond, wholly other. His ways are not our ways, neither are His thoughts our thoughts. Betwixt God and man is an unfathomable gulf that man cannot bridge; so Job calls for an Arbiter, who can come between God and man, and

lay His hands upon both. If only there were such an Arbiter,
he sobs, then I could speak, with the confidence that God hears.

> He is not a man, as I am, that I should   9:32
>   answer Him,
>   and we should come together in judgment.
> Neither is there an Arbiter betwixt us,   9:33
>   that might lay His hand upon us both.
> Let Him take His rod away from me,   9:34
>   and let not fear of Him terrify me.
> Then would I speak, and not fear Him.   9:35

Job did not have the theology of the Incarnation carefully
worked out in his mind. Indeed, almost two thousand years
after Job's plea was answered, who among us comprehends
the mystery of the God-sent Arbiter? Job asks that the Arbiter
take away the rod. He does not envision the unthinkable
mystery that, "with His stripes we are healed." Job prays that
God may understand. God answered the prayer by coming
down into the ditch with Job.

(9:33 presents a minor problem in translation. The Authorized Version speaks of a "daysman." Since this term expresses nothing to the reader today, a change is called for.
The Revised Standard Version reads: "umpire." Though the
term is perfectly intelligible, it is not sublime, and does not
belong in the poem. "Mediator" expresses almost exactly
what the Hebrew noun implies. But this word suggests more
to a Christian than is implied in Job. So I thought it best to
substitute a theologically neutral word, "arbiter." Though
this term is not sublime either, at least it evokes visions of
a law court, and not a ball game.)

Job has charged that God does not hear, yet he continues
to call upon God. We can see that his cry for Christ was
a blinding flash of light. But to Job the thought was one
more despair piled upon despair. An arbiter is needed, and
there is no arbiter.

Weary of life, Job gives free course to his bitterness. His
cry goes up, "My God, my God, why?" The prayer is not
defiant, but one of helpless reproach, the wail of a child
abandoned by his father. God created Job, and led him to
believe that God is good. God knows that Job has been up-

right. God is almighty, and Job suffers. The thought again is more of a whimper than a roar, God, why don't You leave me alone? Once more Job looks into Sheol, and finds it a land where even the light is as darkness.

Thou huntest me as a fierce lion;	10:16b
Thou renewest Thy witnesses against me,	10:17
and increasest Thine indignation upon me;	
changes and war are against me.	
Wherefore then hast Thou brought me forth	10:18
out of the womb?	
Oh that I had given up the ghost,	
and no eye had seen me!	
I should have been as though I had not been;	10:19
I should have been carried from the womb	
to the grave.	
Are not my days few?	10:20
cease then, and let me alone,	
that I may take comfort a little,	
Before I go whence I shall not return,	10:21
even to the land of darkness and the	
shadow of death;	
A land of darkness, as darkness itself;	10:22
and of the shadow of death, without any order,	
and where the light is as darkness.	

FIRST SPEECH OF ZOPHAR 11:1-20

Job's reply to Bildad evidently has convinced Zophar that there is no use being tactful. Where Bildad scourged with whips, Zophar uses scorpions.

Should not the multitude of words be answered?	11:2
and should a man full of talk be justified?	
Should thy lies make men hold their peace?	11:3
and when thou mockest, shall no man	
make thee ashamed?	
For thou hast said, "My doctrine is pure,"	11:4
and "I am clean in Thine eyes."	
But oh that God would speak,	11:5
and open His lips against thee;	

And that He would shew thee the secrets   11:6a
  of wisdom,
    that they are double to that which is!

When Zophar's wish was fulfilled, and God did indeed open
His lips and speak, then Job's problem was solved, and the
Satan's question triumphantly answered, though not exactly
as Zophar had anticipated. 11:6a means that the things hidden
from human knowledge are far more than the things known.
This is a valued truth in science today, as well as faith.
Men easily say that God's way is mystery. But many, like
Zophar, are quite confident of their ability to understand
what is obscure to others.

Zophar gives a splendid illustration of his penetrating
insight.

Know therefore that God exacteth of thee   11:6b
  less than thine iniquity deserveth.

Such a remark might have considerable value, if spoken
while looking into a mirror. But from a man who is not
suffering, to a man who is suffering, this remark is cruel
and utterly heartless, of no possible benefit to the sufferer.
As A. S. Peake comments:

> The suggestion that God is forgetful of a portion of Job's sin,
> does not remember it all against him, and therefore that his
> suffering is less than what he might justly have received, is not
> too rancorous for Zophar, the coarsest of the friends, though it
> is rather strong even for him at this stage of the debate.

—New Century Bible, *Job,* page 127.

Abstractly, most Christians would agree that none has
earned the love of God, that most deserve censure. The religious problems of divine justice, however, lie not in pale
abstractions, but in human life. Granted that we all have
sinned and fallen short of God's glory, the fact remains that
the sorrows of life are unevenly distributed. Quite frequently
those who deserve it least receive most sorrow. Zophar seems
never to wonder why Zophar is not the man covered with
boils, bereft of his children.

He who can be so profoundly wrong can be profoundly
right:

Canst thou by searching find out God? 11:7
  canst thou find out the Almighty unto perfection?
It is as high as heaven; 11:8
  what canst thou do?
  deeper than Sheol;
  what canst thou know?
The measure thereof is longer than the earth, 11:9
  and broader than the sea.
If He cut off, and shut up, 11:10
  or gather together, then who can hinder Him?

Zophar has asked if Job can, by searching, find out God. He has confidently answered in the negative. But he does not believe that the answer applies to himself. With sure confidence that he understands, where Job does not, he says:

For He knoweth vain men: 11:11
  when He seeth wickedness,
    will He not consider it?
For a vain man would be wise, 11:12
  though man be born like a wild ass's colt.

The expression concerning the wild ass's colt was doubtless a proverb. We cannot be precise about the meaning today, but we can be completely sure that it is not a compliment. The wild ass outdid the domestic variety about ten to one in terms of stubbornness.

To his preternaturally stubborn friend, Zophar concludes with words that sound harsh and grating. Take these words away from Job, and read them in isolation from Zophar's cruelty and Job's anguish. You will find them filled with beauty and truth. Like jewels of gold in a swine's snout, they are sadly out of place. No Christian could argue with the good advice given. Turn to God. If you have done wrong, repent, and God will welcome you back to Himself. When you are in right relations with God, you will know real security. This is a large part of the intellectual content of evangelical Christianity. One cannot impugn Zophar's intellectual orthodoxy. But there is orthodoxy of the heart as well as the head, and Zophar's heart is badly out of tune with God. Where God calls for humility and love, Zophar responds with arrogant

self-righteousness. He pronounces the truth in a manner that
makes it false.

If thou prepare thine heart,	11:13
and stretch out thine hands toward Him;	
If iniquity be in thine hand, put it far away,	11:14
and let not wickedness dwell in thy tabernacles.	
For then shalt thou lift up thy face without spot;	11:15
yea, thou shalt be steadfast, and shalt not fear:	
Because thou shalt forget thy misery,	11:16
and remember it as waters that pass away:	
And thine age shall be clearer than the noon-day;	11:17
thou shalt shine forth,	
thou shalt be as the morning.	
And thou shalt be secure, because there is hope;	11:18
yea, thou shalt dig about thee,	
and thou shalt take thy rest in safety.	
Also thou shalt lie down,	11:19
and none shall make thee afraid;	
yea, many shall make suit unto thee.	
But the eyes of the wicked shall fail,	11:20
and they shall not escape,	
and their hope shall be as the giving up	
of the ghost.	

JOB'S FIRST RESPONSE TO ZOPHAR   12:1–14:22

Sardonically, Job cuts Zophar down to size with the most
humorous verse in the entire Bible:

No doubt but ye are the people,	12:2
and wisdom shall die with you!	

The comforters have stressed the doctrine of material retributive justice, a pious theory that does not fit the world of
actual experience. Job disproves the theory by citing a negative
instance, namely himself. Then he engages in some rather wild
generalizations of his own about the prosperity of the wicked.
He calls upon the forces of nature to testify that God is almighty. What happens in the world takes place because God
ordains it. 12:9b quotes Isaiah 41:20, an intimation that
nature and Scripture alike agree in this, God is all-powerful.

By implication, God could have prevented my tragedy, had He cared.

> I am as one mocked of his neighbor, 12:4
>   who called upon God, and He answered me;
>   the just upright man is laughed to scorn.

> The tabernacles of robbers prosper, 12:6
>   and they that provoke God are secure;
>   into whose hand God bringeth abundantly.
> But ask now the beasts, and they shall teach thee; 12:7
>   and the fowls of the air, and they shall tell thee:
> Or speak to the earth, and it shall teach thee; 12:8
>   and the fishes of the sea shall declare unto thee.
> Who knoweth not in all these 12:9
>   that the hand of the Lord hath wrought this?
> In whose hand is the soul of every living thing, 12:10
>   and the breath of all mankind.

The chapter concludes with some dark and horrible words, as Job avers that the world shows God's power, but not His justice. Verses 12 and 13, of course, are intended sarcastically. In the former Job sneers at his comforters, in the latter at God.

> With the ancient is wisdom; 12:12
>   and in length of days understanding.
> With Him is wisdom and strength, 12:13
>   He hath counsel and understanding.
> Behold, He breaketh down, 12:14
>   and it cannot be built again;
> He shutteth up a man,
>   and there can be no opening.
> Behold, He withholdeth the waters, 12:15
>   and they dry up;
> also He sendeth them out, and they
>   overturn the earth.
> With Him is strength and wisdom: 12:16
>   the deceived and the deceiver are His.
> He leadeth counsellors away spoiled, 12:17
>   and maketh the judges fools.

> He removeth away the speech of the trusty, 12:20
>   and taketh away the understanding of the aged.

> He taketh away the heart of the chief of the people   12:24
>   of the earth,
>   and causeth them to wander in a wilderness
>   where there is no way.
> They grope in the dark without light,   12:25
>   and He maketh them to stagger like a
>   drunken man.

Job savagely shifts the attack against those who have striven
to prove the justice of God by argument from the facts of
experience. As Job has said, they have not stated the facts
correctly. It is a truism of logic that from a false premise
any conclusion can be drawn. That the good always prosper
and the wicked always suffer is a false premise. Surely faith
must be based on firmer ground than this.

> I desire to reason with God.   13:3
> But ye are forgers of lies,   13:4
>   ye are all physicians of no value.
> Oh that ye would altogether hold your peace!   13:5
>   and it should be your wisdom.
> Hear now my reasoning,   13:6
>   and hearken to the pleadings of my lips.
> Will ye speak wickedly for God?   13:7
>   and talk deceitfully for Him?
> Will ye show Him favor?   13:8
>   Will ye plead the case for God?
> Would it be good that He should search you out?   13:9
>   or as one man mocketh another, do ye so
>   mock Him?
> He will surely reprove you,   13:10
>   if ye do secretly show favor.

Job's attitude has been called "magnificent inconsistency."
He has denied that God is just. Yet he warns the comforters
to beware God's justice. He pricks to the heart of all smug
and easy-going faith that reaches admirable results by denying the unpleasant facts. A lie in defense of God is still a lie.
Job's heart cries out for the living God, and his comforters
offer him platitudinous half-truths. The violence of Job's
protest shows that he is not so far from God as he thinks.

As the comforters have been persistent in maintaining Job's wickedness, he has been equally persistent in upholding his own integrity. Now he announces to them that he will issue a challenge to God,

> Hold your peace, let me alone, that I may speak,   13:13
>   and let come on me what will.
> Wherefore? I will take my flesh in my teeth,   13:14
>   and put my life in my hand.
> Behold He will slay me, I have no hope;   13:15
>   but I will maintain mine own ways before Him.

The translation differs significantly from the Authorized Version:

> Though He slay me, yet will I trust in Him.   13:15

It is a difficult verse to translate with assurance. There are two different Hebrew words pronounced "lo." One means "him," the other means "not." I have followed the Masoretic Text, which reads "not." In this instance the translators of the King James Version followed a marginal note, which reads "Him." They produced a glorious declaration of faith that is out of place at this stage of Job's spiritual growth. Here he is still trusting, hopelessly, in his own power to save himself.

Job implies broadly that the comforters are hypocrites, and that he is not. If you have any experience at all with church work, you have heard this sad old refrain many times. It might be called Standard Defense #17-B against the gospel of Christ: There are too many hypocrites in church, and if there's one thing I can't stand, it's a hypocrite. It is hard, often, to keep from laughing at people who make this complacent judgment of themselves. At least Job could back up his claim with moral performance. But he does not ask, yet, the fundamental question, Is my morality worth enough to purchase God's love?

> This also shall be my salvation,   13:16
>   that a hypocrite cannot come before Him.

The Apostle Paul quotes 3:16a in Philippians 1:19. The letter to the Philippians, you remember, was written while Paul was in prison awaiting the court's decision. If the

decision is favorable to his case, he will walk away a free man.
If the decision goes against him, he will be executed. The
epistle, written under these trying circumstances, has rightly
been called the happiest letter ever written. A comparison
between Job and Paul is inevitable. Both suffered cruel un-
merited griefs, but there is all the difference in the world
between their responses to sorrow. This difference, and the
reason for it, has nowhere been better described than by
Carroll E. Simcox:

> What makes the difference between the two faithful sufferers?
> Only one thing, but it makes an infinite difference: the cross
> of Jesus Christ. Paul sees God Himself taking the pain of the
> world as His own. Job sees God sitting, serene and untouched,
> above the water-floods of woe. And this, to him, is the scandal
> and the perplexity. If God, yea, *since* God is good, just, and
> all-powerful, why does He let His faithful children fall into
> such terrible pits of disaster? This is Job's question, to which
> he finds no answer. Paul does not even ask the question and
> he does not hunger for the answer. He has reflected upon the
> mystery, but because he sees God in Christ, coming into the
> pain of our flesh to redeem it, he is concerned with making
> use of his tribulations for the extension of God's victory rather
> than with reconciling the fact of evil with the fact of God's
> goodness.

—They Met At Philippi, page 2.

Turning from the comforters, Job challenges God direct,
offering to appear in court either as plaintiff or defendant.
He asks that God withdraw His afflicting hand, and refrain
from terrifying Job by His almighty power.

Only do not two things unto me;	13:20
then will I not hide myself from Thee.	
Withdraw Thine hand far from me;	13:21
and let not Thy dread make me afraid:	
Then call Thou, and I will answer;	13:22
or let me speak, and answer Thou me.	

God is silent. Job begins his plea by demanding to know
the sins of which he is accused. Almost as a parenthesis in
his demand is his statement of the sixth, and most terrible,
of the scourges that have come upon him. He has lost God.
It is one thing to be angry with God. This Job has done,
quite competently. It is another, and even worse, to seek God

and find Him not. The condition is called "aridity" in the language of devotion. It comes to the most saintly, I do not know why.

I do not propose that Job was driven into the arid God-less waste as punishment for his sins. If only the sinless could pray, there would be little praying in this world. In what follows, I shall suggest, from time to time, that Job's pride keeps him isolated from God longer than might have been the case with a more humble man. But I do not imply, here or elsewhere, that Job is punished for the sin of pride by any of his six agonies; material loss, the death of his children, sickness, betrayal by his wife, the comforters, or—worst of all—his spiritual aridity. At a time when he most needs God, he cannot find Him.

For an excellent analysis of aridity, I turn to Georgia Harkness:

> Spiritual dryness....means the sense of spiritual frustration, barrenness, and loneliness that comes to one who after having prayed effectively for years now finds himself unable to do so. It is the darkness of spirit and emptiness of soul that ensues when one feels as if something had snapped in his religious life and his prayers now reach no further than his own lips. To the spiritually sensitive person, this loss of a sense of divine companionship is an acutely unhappy experience. Often it is joined with an exaggerated self-pity or self-accusation and with deep depression about life in general.
>
> —*Prayer and The Common Life*, page 111.

Admitting the minor sins of his youth, Job can think of none that will account for his six-fold calamity. It seems that Job shares, to a considerable degree, the comforters' theology, that suffering is necessarily a punishment for sin.

How many are my iniquities and sins?	13:23
make me to know my transgression and my sin.	
Wherefore hidest Thou Thy face,	13:24
and holdest me for Thine enemy?	
Wilt Thou break a leaf driven to and fro?	13:25
and wilt Thou pursue the dry stubble?	
For Thou writest bitter things against me,	13:26
and makest me to possess the iniquities	
of my youth.	

The challenge continues in a plaint of haunting pathos about man's condition on earth, in which Job compares man's life with the swift-fading beauty of the flower. He is as transitory as the shadow. And will God contend with such?

Man that is born of a woman is of few days,   14:1
    and full of trouble.
He cometh forth like a flower, and is cut down: 14:2
    he fleeth also as a shadow, and continueth not.
And dost Thou open Thine eyes upon such a one,   14:3
    and bringest me into judgment with Thee?
Who can bring a clean thing out of an unclean?   14:4
    not one.
Seeing his days are determined,   14:5
    the number of his months are with Thee,
    Thou hast appointed his bounds that
      he cannot pass.
Turn from him, that he may rest,   14:6
    till he shall accomplish, as a hireling, his day.

The remainder of the plaint concerns man's state after death. Job renews his fascinated examination of a possible after-life, only to reject the idea once more. This is Job's most clearcut and specific denial of all that we Christians believe about eternal life. Accordingly, it behooves us to look carefully, to see if perhaps there is here something more than mere negation.

For there is hope of a tree,   14:7
    if it be cut down,
    that it will sprout again,
    and that the tender branch thereof
      will not cease.
Though the root thereof wax old in the earth,   14:8
    and the stock thereof die in the ground;
Yet through the scent of water it will bud,   14:9
    and bring forth boughs like a plant.
But man dieth, and wasteth away;   14:10
    yea, man giveth up the ghost, and where is he?
As the waters fail from the sea,   14:11
    and the flood decayeth and drieth up;

> So man lieth down, and riseth not: 14:12
> till the heavens be no more, they shall not awake,
> nor be raised out of their sleep.

A principle of logic may apply at this and several other points in the Book of Job. The principle is known as *reductio ad absurdum*. In untechnical language, it means taking a premise and following it through to a conclusion. If the conclusion is irrational, then either the premise or the reasoning is wrong. This logical principle was isolated and labelled by Greek and Roman philosophers, who had almost no bearing upon Hebrew thought. But straight thinking is the prerogative of every race. A Hebrew poet could well use the *reductio ad absurdum* without calling it by that name.

The major premise is that death means the end. The minor premise is that in God's world the joys and sorrows of life are distributed with little regard for the moral worth of the individual. The conclusion—which is usually credited to Epictetus—is a quandary: God is not just, God is not almighty, or there is no God. Since there is something radically wrong with the conclusion, one may well question the major premise, since only a person as blind as the comforters could question the minor premise or the reasoning.

Job knew the dilemma as well as did Epictetus. As yet, he does not seriously question his denial of immortality. But he will not quite curse God and die. His heart longs to believe that after death he may see God, face to face. His mind rejects the belief. Before Job saw the light, he stumbled in darkness. His stumblings are recorded in order that you might think deeply about the fundamental relationship between love and life.

Job's doubt cannot keep him from reflecting upon the possibility that his mind rejects. The logic of faith will not permit one to accept forever the discordant beliefs that God is love and that man's goal is the grave. So Job toys, hopelessly, with the thought that after a sleep of death he may know life.

> Oh, that Thou wouldest hide me in Sheol, 14:13
> that Thou wouldest keep me secret,

until Thy wrath be passed,
   that Thou wouldest appoint me a set time,
   and remember me.
If a man die, shall he live again?   14:14
   All the days of my appointed time would I wait,
   till my relief should come.
Thou wouldest call, and I would answer Thee: 14:15
   Thou wouldest long for the work of Thy hands.

The thought of God calling and Job responding joyfully is too much. Job's mind rejects what his heart demands—and rightly so. The logic of faith cannot, by itself, undo the fact of sin. Without the mediating work of Christ, how can any of us, even a man as righteous as Job, think of dwelling eternally in the love of God. Who has earned such a privilege? What right have we to lay hold on eternal life? We have only the right of those for whom Christ laid His life down. And Job, during his life on earth, did not know Christ.

The waters wear the stones;   14:19
   Thou washest away the things which grow out
     of the dust of the earth;
   and Thou destroyest the hope of man.
Thou prevailest for ever against him,   14:20
   and he passeth:
   Thou changest his countenance, and sendest
    him away.
His sons come to honor, and he knoweth it not; 14:21
   and they are brought low, but he perceiveth
    it not.

IV. THE SECOND CYCLE OF SPEECHES   15:1—21:34

A. Second speech of Eliphaz   15:1-35
1. The wickedness of Job   15:1-16
2. The fate of the wicked   15:17-35

B. Job's second response to Eliphaz   16:1—17:16
1. The sorry comforters   16:1-5
2. Job's pitiable state   16:6-17
3. The Witness in Heaven   16:18—17:5
4. The brother of the worm   17:6-16

C. Second speech of Bildad   18:1-21
1. Defense of the comforters   18:1-4
2. The fate of the wicked   18:5-21

D. Job's second response to Bildad   19:1-29
1. The enmity of God   19:1-12
2. The enmity of man   19:13-24
3. The indestructible confidence in God   19:25-29

E. Second speech of Zophar   20:1-29
1. The triumph of the wicked is short   20:1-21
2. The doom of the wicked is certain   20:22-29

F. Job's second response to Zophar   21:1-34
1. The prosperity of the wicked   21:1-21
2. The dark mysteries of Providence   21:22-34

The Second Cycle of Speeches 15:1—21:34

In the second cycle of speeches the comforters say again, and with even greater frankness, what they have so capably expressed before. The wicked are punished, the righteous are blessed, hence Job is wicked. As Job stubbornly maintains his integrity, the comforters with equal stubbornness maintain their argument. But as Job develops through his inward struggle, they become less and less tolerant. The reader is apt to grow weary of their repeated emphasis upon what they have already emphasized. But the inspired writer had a purpose in mind. He intended to expose the hollowness of the popular faith in material retributive justice, and no one could say that he failed in this. He expressed with vivid insight and keen logic a faith that was inadequate for his day, and is inadequate for ours. If it sounds flat and unconvincing when stated by Eliphaz, Bildad, and Zophar, has the passage of the centuries improved it greatly? Is success a reward for piety, and failure the inevitable result of impiety? Do we worship God for the trinkets that fall from His hand, or for the sake of God alone? Doth man worship God for nought?

SECOND SPEECH OF ELIPHAZ (15:1-35)

With considerable accuracy, Eliphaz accuses Job of pride:

Art thou the first man that was born?	15:7
or wast thou made before the hills?	
What knowest thou, that we know not?	15:9
what understandest thou, which is not in us?	
Are the consolations of God small with thee?	15:11
is there any secret thing with thee?	

The last verse has given translators much difficulty. At least one possible meaning is that Job has been ungrateful for the blessings of divine Providence, so ungrateful that he has even rejected the wise and gentle words of the comforters. If this be the meaning it sounds strange from the lips of one who has accused another of pride.

Unconscious that he is talking in circles, Eliphaz stresses once more the inevitability of sin and the doom of the wicked. It is not clear why he considers himself among the undoomed. In his second speech, Eliphaz fails to hold out any ray of hope to Job. There is not a word about man's repentance and God's love, only a gloomy reiteration of the divine wrath against sinful man.

> What is man, that he should be clean?   15:14
>   and he which is born of a woman,
>   that he should be righteous?
> Behold, He putteth no trust in His saints;   15:15
>   yea, the heavens are not clean in His sight;
> How much more abominable and filthy is man,   15:16
>   which drinketh iniquity like water?

> The wicked man travaileth with pain all his days,   15:20
>   and the number of years is hidden to the oppressor.

> For he stretcheth out his hand against God,   15:25
>   and strengtheneth himself against the Almighty.

JOB'S SECOND RESPONSE TO ELIPHAZ   16:1–17:16

When Eliphaz has expressed morbid thoughts in sonorous rhetoric and dignified tones, Job responds crisply:

> I have heard many such things: 16:2
>   miserable comforters are ye all.

> I also could speak as ye do: 16:4
>   if your soul were in my soul's stead,
> I could heap up words against you,
>   and shake my head at you.
> But I would strengthen you with my mouth,   16:5
>   and the moving of my lips should assuage
>   your grief.

Job's confidence in his ability as a counsellor may be forgiven in view of the circumstances. Would the story have been much different if Eliphaz were the afflicted and Job the comforter? I doubt it. Some human problems will respond only to a divine solution, and Job's was such.

In the lurid description of his fate that follows, there is a suggestion that Job has begun to suspect the Satan's part in his tribulations. Job is alienated from his friends. He knows the crushing weight of loneliness. And worst, he believes that God too has forsaken him.

> Thou hast filled me with wrinkles,   16:8
> > which is a witness against me:
> and my leanness rising up in me beareth witness
> > to my face.
> He teareth me in his wrath, who hateth me: 16:9
> > he gnasheth upon me with his teeth;
> > mine enemy sharpeneth his eyes upon me.
> They have gaped upon me with their mouth;   16:10
> > they have smitten me upon the cheek
> > reproachfully;
> > they have gathered themselves together against me.
> God hath delivered me to the ungodly,   16:11
> > and turned me over into the hands of the wicked.
>
> His archers compass me round about,   16:13
> > He cleaveth my reins asunder, and doth not spare;
> > He poureth out my gall upon the ground.
>
> My face is foul with weeping,   16:16
> > and on my eyelids is the shadow of death;
> Though there is no injustice in mine hands   16:17
> > and my prayer is pure.

We sometimes sing of the "love that wilt not let me go." Job is about as far from conscious recognition of that love as man can get. He has practically accused God of being a murderer. It seems that he is on the verge of accepting his wife's admonition, "Curse God and die." And yet, with illogical tenacity, he clings to his integrity, his life, and God.

> O earth, cover not thou my blood,   16:18
> > and let my cry have no place.

These cryptic words are explained usually as a reference to

the Hebrew laws of revenge. Blood not covered with earth was understood to have been violently shed. It called for vengeance upon the murderer. (See Genesis 4:10 and Ezekiel 24:7.) But it is more probable that these words are a prayer for life. Do not let me sink into the earth. Let my cry for justice continue until it is heard. And Job voices his confidence that the cry is heard.

> Even now, behold, my Witness is in heaven,   16:19
> and my record is on high.
> And since my friends scorn me: 16:20
> mine eye poureth out tears unto God.
> Oh that He might plead for a man with God,   16:21
> as a man pleadeth for his neighbor!
> When a few years are come,   16:22
> then I shall go the way whence I shall not return.

A furious debate rages about the witness in heaven. Some claim that the witness cannot be God; for God is already witness, as well as being prosecutor and judge and executioner. Their explanation of the alternative is less than satisfactory. One may ask, "If it be not He, who then is it?"

The Hebrew word translated "witness" has no real equivalent in English. Perhaps "sponsor" is the closest to its meaning. It means not merely one who knows that the accused is innocent, but one who will see that this innocence is recognized. Job appeals from God who has stricken him to God as he has known Him in the past, just, kind, loving.

No longer does Job believe that he will receive justice on earth. Not yet has he seen the light of life after physical death. But still he fights for justice. He is not battling now for survival, only for the final recognition, in heaven, that Job was a righteous man. He has already cried that God is his sponsoring Witness. Now he calls upon God to be his Bondsman.

> My spirit is consumed, my days are extinct,   17:1
> the grave is ready for me.
> Are there not mockers with me?   17:2
> and doth not mine eye continue in their
> provocation?
> Give now a pledge, be surety for me with Thyself;   17:3
> who else is there that will strike hands with me?

> For Thou hast hid their heart from understanding: 17:4
>   therefore shalt Thou not exalt them.

Since the comforters cannot understand, they will not offer to provide bail for Job's appearance in court and his final vindication. So Job turns to God, asking that He provide the bail. In the Book of Proverbs, you read frequently about striking hands as a sign that an agreement is ratified. No man will strike hands with Job to guarantee his appearance at the longed-for trial. God who is the Judge must provide the bail, and when the case comes up, long after Job's death, the divine Bondsman will be the sponsoring Witness.

Once again the sufferer who has seen a momentary light lapses back into utter despair, calling himself brother to the worm.

> Mine eye also is dim by reason of sorrow, 17:7
>   and all my members are as a shadow.

> If I wait, Sheol is mine house: 17:13
>   I have made my bed in the darkness.
> I have said to corruption, "Thou art my father," 17:14
>   to the worm, "Thou art my mother,
>   and my sister."
> And where is now my hope? 17:15
>   as for my hope, who shall see it?
> They shall go down to the bars of Sheol, 17:16
>   when our rest together is in the dust.

SECOND SPEECH OF BILDAD 18:1-21

Bildad's second speech outdoes all previous efforts in the lurid description of the fate that befalls the wicked. He makes it abundantly clear that Job is the wicked man God has in mind for a horrible end. A few words will suffice:

> Terrors shall make him afraid on every side 18:11
>   and shall drive him to his feet.
> His strength shall be hunger-bitten, 18:12
>   and destruction shall be ready at his side.
> It shall devour the strength of his skin: 18:13
>   even the first-born of death shall devour his
>   strength.

| His confidence shall be rooted out of his | 18:14 |
| tabernacle, | |

and it shall bring him to the king of terrors.

| It shall dwell in his tabernacle, | 18:15 |
| because it is none of his: | |

brimstone shall be scattered upon his habitation.

| Surely such are the dwellings of the wicked, | 18:21 |

and this is the place of him that knoweth not God.

JOB'S SECOND RESPONSE TO BILDAD   19:1-29

When Bildad has vividly described the fate of the wicked, Job responds with considerable heat:

| If indeed ye will magnify yourselves against me, | **19:5** |
| and plead against me my reproach; | |

| Know now that God hath overthrown me, | **19:6** |
| and hath compassed me with His net. | |

Magnifying one's self against another probably means the age-old practice of building up a high opinion of oneself by tearing down someone else. Job, with reason, accuses his comforters of doing just this, as he repeats his cry about the enmity of God. From this he turns to bewail the hostility of his friends:

| My breath is abhorred by my wife, | 19:17 |
| and I am loathsome to the children of my tribe. | |

| All my inward friends abhor me; | 19:19 |
| and they whom I loved are turned against me. | |

| My bone cleaveth to my skin and to my flesh, | 19:20 |
| and I am escaped with the skin of my teeth. | |

| Have pity upon me, have pity upon me, | 19:21 |
| O ye my friends; | |

for the hand of God hath touched me.

| Why do ye persecute me as God, | 19:22 |
| and are not satisfied with my flesh? | |

Though he has scourged his comforters, Job calls upon them for pity. But he gives the hand of God as the reason for their pity, and this is the cause of their hostility. How should these,

intent upon flattering God, sympathize with one whom God
has smitten?

Job has turned from God to man. And man has failed him.
Now Job calls upon posterity to examine his cause, momen-
tarily confident that later generations would acclaim him a
righteous man, if they could have access to the facts.

> Oh that my words were now written!   19:23
>   Oh that they were printed in a book!
> That they were graven with an iron pen   19:24
>   and lead in the rock forever!

The appeal to living man has failed. The appeal to the
future is wistful and hopeless. Then comes a blinding flash
of light:

> For I know that my Redeemer liveth,   19:25
>   and that He shall stand at the latter day upon
>   the earth:
> And after my skin has been destroyed,   19:26
>   then without my flesh I shall see God:
> Whom I shall see for myself,   19:27
>   and mine eyes shall behold, and not another;
>   my heart is consumed within me.

The fever is broken, the crisis is past. Job remains a desper-
ately sick man, spiritually and physically. Before him lies a
painful convalescence. But the worst of his illness is behind
him.

As frequently happens when one encounters a flash of light
in the midst of intense darkness, one is at first more confused
than helped. Job's emotion is so intense that his heart (kid-
neys in Hebrew) is consumed. But what is the emotion about?

The term "redeemer," with its derivative "redemption,"
like many other important theological terms in the Bible, is
derived from a Hebrew social custom, not from a philosophic
abstraction. If a man sold himself into slavery, a kinsman was
obligated to be his redeemer. In the Book of Ruth, the closest
relative was unable to redeem Naomi's land and to marry
Ruth. Since he could not do this, he transferred his respon-
sibilities to Boaz, who became the redeemer. When a person
was slain, a kinsman had a duty to exact crude vengeance

against the murderer's family. This person was the redeemer. By extension, then, a redeemer is one who defends the oppressed.

(The term "redeemer" has acquired new and glorious Christian connotations. Yet it remains the best possible translation of an Old Testament term. The closest substitute would be "vindicator." But the redeemer's function was essentially one of love, even in its harshest aspects, while a vindicator's is essentially one of law.)

No earthly redeemer is living to defend Job. His sons are dead, and his other relatives have deserted him. Does Job then refer to God as his Redeemer? Is he merely hoping that some day, after Job's death, God will proclaim Job's righteousness to the world? Before now, Job has expressed his confidence in the heavenly sponsoring Witness, and has called for the Arbiter, who will stand betwixt God and man, and lay hands upon both.

With the wisdom of hindsight, it is easy for us Christians to see that Job is calling for one fully God and fully man, to bear his griefs and carry his sorrows. Centuries later, Anselm of Canterbury in his profound work, *Cur Deus Homo?* showed by rigid logic that, since God is God, there must be an Incarnation. Job is not a theologian sitting in his study and theorizing about God. He is a man lost and bewildered, who sees a flash of light, and cries, "My Redeemer liveth." Again one asks: If it is not God, who then is it?

There is probably more scholarly disagreement about 19:26 than about any other verse in the entire Book of Job. All translators have had grave difficulty with it. The Authorized Version inserts three words, others have tugged and hauled as best they could to reach an intelligible meaning. The question is: Does Job expect to see his Redeemer while he is living on earth or following his death?

In the early centuries of Christian thought, Origen claimed that in this place Job sees a glimpse of heaven, a life after earthly life. Chrysostom refuted Origen, pointing out that Job denies the possibility in 14:12 ff. And ever since the Christian commentators have been siding with one or the other. Much as I admire Chrysostom, it seems to me that in this instance his reasoning is poor. Job could have changed his mind. Those who are convinced that there is here no glimpse of eternal life seems very positive about it. With considerable diffidence, recognizing that I disagree with many, it still seems to me that here Job has a presentiment, however vague, that following his physical death he will enter into the presence of God. And, quite rightly, at the prospect his heart is consumed within him.

Job's brief moment of exultation is followed by a swift relapse into bitterness. He who has so exulted in the final triumph of his Redeemer turns savagely against his comforters. We may imagine that they were shocked by his wild claims, and that they made threatening gestures of interruption. Job says with menace:

> If ye say, "How will we persecute him?"   19:28
>   seeing the root of the matter is found in me;
> Be ye afraid of the sword;   19:29
>   for wrath bringeth the punishments of the sword,
>   that ye may know there is a judgment.

Job who has so heatedly denied God's justice affirms that it is a factor to be reckoned with. His anger against those who are trying to help is exactly what one might expect from a tortured human being. Not yet has Job heard the Voice from the Whirlwind. Not yet is he ready to intercede in prayer for those who have added to his torment. For the moment, he is angry that they do not share his glimpse of the divine Redeemer, and he threatens that one of a redeemer's functions is to wield the avenging sword.

SECOND SPEECH OF ZOPHAR 20:1-29

Zophar clings to the precious jewel of consistency, announcing with firm determination that the triumph of the wicked is short, and their doom is sure.

> The triumphing of the wicked is short,   20:5
>   and the joy of the hypocrite but for a moment.
> Though his excellency mount up to the heavens,   20:6
>   and his head reach unto the clouds;
> Yet he shall perish forever like his own dung.   20:7a
>
> The heavens shall reveal his iniquity;   20:27
>   and the earth shall rise up against him.

> The increase of his house shall depart,   20:28
>   and his goods shall flow away
>   in the day of His wrath.
> This is the portion of a wicked man from God,   20:29
>   and the heritage appointed unto him by God.

JOB'S SECOND RESPONSE TO ZOPHAR   21:1-34

Vividly has Zophar depicted the downfall of the wicked.
Job contradicts him. Material retributive justice does not
hold in this world.

> Wherefore do the wicked live,   21:7
>   become old, yea, are mighty in power?
>
> Their houses are safe from fear,   21:9
>   neither is the rod of God upon them.
> Their bull gendereth, and faileth not;   21:10
>   their cow calveth, and casteth not her calf.
> They send forth their little ones like a flock,   21:11
>   and their children dance.
>
> They spend their days in wealth,   21:13
>   and in peace go down to Sheol.
> Therefore, they say unto God: "Depart from us;   21:14
>   for we desire not the knowledge of Thy ways.
> What is the Almighty, that we should serve Him?   21:15
>   and what profit should we have,
>   if we pray unto Him?"
> Lo, their good is not in their hand: 21:16
>   the counsel of the wicked is far from me.

Were this a sociological treatise, one would point out that
the way of the wicked is not always so smooth as Job has
indicated. But he is cutting to the heart of the matter. The
issue is man's relationship with God, not prosperity, ease, and
comfort. What is the profit of prayer? Coverdale, the six-
teenth century translator, expresses the thought vividly, "What
maner of felowe is the Almightie that we shulde serve Him?"
Do we pray in order to profit? Is our devotion the nickel we
put into the cosmic slot machine, that we may withdraw the
fulfillment of our own desires? Does "the coin of faith de-

mand the chocolate bar of material benefit?" (V. E. Reichert, *Job,* page 110).

The comforters have attempted to tailor the facts of human experience to fit their theology, much as, in more recent years, some Christians have denied scientific evidence in conflict with their understanding of Christian faith. (This seems a curious way to defend the Lord of Truth.) Those who deny fact in the interest of dogma are committing the sin of presumption. By insisting upon the principle of material retributive justice, while facing a massive negation of that principle, the comforters are in effect telling God how He ought to order the world, not noticing the way He does order it. And Job wearily asks the comforters to face some unpleasant facts.

> Ye say, "God layeth up iniquity for his children!" 21:19
>   let Him reward the wicked himself,
>   that he may know it.
> Let his own eyes see his destruction, 21:20
>   and let him drink of the wrath of the Almighty.
> For what pleasure hath he in his house after him, 21:21
>   when the number of his months is cut off
>   in the midst?
> Shall any teach God knowledge? 21:22
>   seeing He judgeth those that are high.
> One dieth in his full strength, 21:23
>   being wholly at ease and quiet.
>
> And another dieth in the bitterness of his soul, 21:25
>   and never eateth with pleasure.
> They shall lie down alike in the dust 21:26
>   and the worms shall cover them.

The second cycle closes on this note of defiance. Job has produced facts. His comforters have produced theories. And Job spurns the theories, saying:

> How then comfort ye me in vain? 21:34
>   In your answers there remaineth but falsehood.

The Third Cycle of Speeches 22:1—27:23

Even a casual reading of the third cycle will convince most that something has happened to the script. We have become accustomed to the order, Eliphaz, Job, Bildad, Job, Zophar, Job. In the third cycle, Zophar speaks not at all. Bildad's speech is remarkably brief, for one whose controlling passion has not been brevity. And Job makes remarks that would come more naturally from Zophar or Bildad. Following hard upon the third cycle (or possibly included in it), comes the incomparable Hymn on Wisdom, which, by our canons of taste, does not fit properly into the Book at this particular point.

It is dangerous at best to reconstruct what took place centuries ago. It seems quite possible, however, that the original poet completed the third cycle of speeches, with Job responding duly to Bildad, Zophar's speech, and Job's conclusion. We know that Job was capable of some fierce and unrestrained language in speaking about God as well as about his fellow man. He has denied that there is any divine justice in the world. He has likened God to a savage hunter stalking his prey. He has contrasted God with a marksman, using Job for the target. With these things in mind, many students believe that in the original version of the third cycle, Job's remarks grew wilder and more fierce than any that had gone before. So rash and outspoken were his words that the editor deleted some, rearranged some, and added the Hymn on Wisdom to bring a touch of quiet beauty in place of strident clamor.

Following this thought through to its conclusion, *The Interpreters' Bible* suggests: "Any restoration of the original text remains conjectural, but the following is the most simple and probable:

    Eliphaz: 22:1-30
    Job: 23:1—24:17; 25

Bildad:	25:1-6; 26:5-14
Job:	26:1-4; 27:1-12
Zophar:	24:18-24; 27:13-23

Thus restored, each discourse yields excellent sense, fits the positions of the respective speakers, and presents satisfactory sequence of ideas" (Volume III, *Job,* page 888).

On the other hand, we are examining the canonical Book of Job, that was constructed under the guidance of the Holy Spirit, and brought into our lives by divine Providence. Christians recognize that many biblical books went through a period of development before reaching the canonical form. (See Jeremiah 36, for example.) Fascinating as the task of reconstruction always is, it remains a hazardous science. The third cycle as we have it today presents a rebel who has passed the peak of his rebellion. He has entered a period of comparative contemplation. His rebellion does not grow until it is shattered by the Voice from the Whirlwind. Rather Job begins, more and more, to see the light of God shining steadily through the thick darkness. This is not to suggest that Job has become meek and humble. But in the third cycle of speeches, he is more restrained than he was in the second. He is far more ready to hear the Voice of God.

The third cycle contains some of the most beautiful poetry in the entire Book of Job. Many deep theological insights are found in this cycle. It would never do to become so absorbed in critical questions about the section that one fails to appreciate the glories in it.

THIRD SPEECH OF ELIPHAZ   22:1-30

While Job has passed the peak of his frenzy, the comforters still are mounting up. Eliphaz has long forgotten the courtly consideration he showed for Job's feelings as he began to comfort him. He ignores most of what Job has said, and picks out one point of attack—Job's insistence that God owes him justice. Eliphaz again "exalts" God to a place where He is indifferent to Job's struggles.

Can a man be profitable unto God?   22:2
   He that is wise is profitable unto himself.

> Is it any pleasure to the Almighty that thou 22:3
> art righteous?
> or is it gain to Him if thou makest thy ways
> blameless?
> Is it because thou fearest Him that He 22:4
> reproveth thee?
> and entereth into judgment with thee?

Following the same remorseless logic, Eliphaz argues that since Job suffers he must be a sinner. Why God, who apparently is indifferent to good, should be concerned about evil is not made clear. Since Job has denied that he is a sinner, Eliphaz proceeds to invent sins which, were Job guilty, would have been grievous indeed.

> Is not thy wickedness great? 22:5
> and thine iniquity infinite?
> For thou hast taken a pledge from thy brother 22:6
> for nought,
> and stripped the naked of their clothing.
> Thou hast not given water to the weary to drink, 22:7
> and thou hast withholden bread from the hungry.
>
> Thou hast sent widows away empty, 22:9
> and the arms of the fatherless have been broken.
> Therefore snares are round about thee, 22:10
> and sudden fear troubleth thee.

Eliphaz continues, using one of the filthiest tricks of debate, that is, quoting someone else almost correctly. 22:13-18 is borrowed from Job's rash and intemperate remarks in chapter 21. Indeed, 22:17-18 are almost direct quotations of 21:14-16. Eliphaz is crowding Job into the corner where he must say, Yes, but. In chapter 21 Job spoke bitterly about the practical atheism of the godless man who prospers. Subtly, Eliphaz identifies Job with the atheist. No reasonable person could deny that Job was impious in what he said. But Eliphaz successfully makes a bad situation worse. Job pointed out that the wicked prosper. Eliphaz glories rather in that they (meaning Job) will be destroyed.

> Is not God in the height of heaven?   22:12
>   and behold the height of the stars,
>   how high they are!
> And thou sayest, "How doth God know?   22:13
>   can He judge through the dark cloud?
> Thick clouds are a covering to Him,   22:14
>   that He seeth not;
> and He walketh in the circuit of heaven."
> Hast thou marked the old way   22:15
>   which wicked men have trodden?
> Which were cut down out of time,   22:16
>   whose foundation was overflown with a flood:
> Which said unto God, "Depart from us:"   22:17
>   and, "What can the Almighty do for us?"
> Yet He filled their houses with good things.   22:18
>   But the counsel of the wicked is far from me.
> The righteous see it, and are glad;   22:19
>   and the innocent laugh them to scorn,
> Saying, "Surely our adversaries are cut off,   22:20
>   and what they left the fire has consumed."

Whether the ensuing words are glorious or horrible depends entirely upon one's understanding of the term "gold." If Eliphaz means the metal with an atomic weight of 197.2, then his statement is the most crass expression of materialism we have yet encountered. On the other hand, gold serves frequently as a symbol for spiritual treasure. Significantly, many Septuagint manuscripts omit 22:24, the verse that is most difficult to "spiritualize." If, as I think, Eliphaz is using "gold" symbolically, then this blind man has, for a moment, seen the truth. The reward of faith is God. To be sure, he still believes in salvation by works. He decrees that when Job has returned to God, once more his prayers will be heard. Once more his desires will be fulfilled. Once more Job will be able to encourage others. And finally, Job will be delivered because his hands once more are clean. Eliphaz relies not upon the forgiving divine nature, but upon the efficacy of Job's repentance.

> Acquaint now thyself with Him, and be at peace: 22:21
>   thereby good shall come unto thee.

Receive, I pray thee, the law from His mouth,   22:22
   and lay up His words in thine heart.

If thou return to the Almighty,   22:23
   thou shalt be built up,
   thou shalt put away iniquity far from thy
   tabernacles.

Then shalt thou lay up gold as dust,   22:24
   and the gold of Ophir as the stones of the brooks.

Yea, the Almighty shall be thy gold,   22:25
   and thy precious silver.

For then shalt thou have thy delight   22:26
   in the Almighty.
   and shalt lift up thy face unto God.

Thou shalt make thy prayer unto Him,   22:27
   and He shall hear thee,
   and thou shalt pay thy vows.

Thou shalt also decree a thing,   22:28
   and it shall be established unto thee:
   and the light shall shine upon thy ways.

When men are cast down, then thou shalt say,   22:29
   "There is lifting up;"
   And He shall save the humble person.

He shall deliver the innocent;   22:30
   and thou shalt be delivered by the pureness of
   thine hands.

JOB'S THIRD RESPONSE TO ELIPHAZ   23:1–24:25

Since Eliphaz has stressed divine transcendence, Job responds with a wistful half-prayer:

Oh that I knew where I might find Him!   23:3
   that I might come even to His seat!

I would order my cause before Him,   23:4
   and fill my mouth with arguments.

I would know the words which He would   23:5
   answer me,
   and understand what He would say unto me.

Behold, I go forward, but He is not there;   23:8
   and backward, but I cannot perceive Him;

> On the left hand I seek Him, but I cannot behold   23:9
>   Him:
> He hideth Himself on the right hand,
>   that I cannot see Him:
> But He knoweth the way that I take: 23:10
>   when He hath tried me, I shall come forth as gold.

One's first response is deep sympathy. But after a time one begins to marvel at the sheer arrogance of a mortal man in suggesting that God is fleeing from His creature. Job hints that God will not let Job find Him; for He knows that Job is innocent, and is ashamed to admit it. Like Martin Luther in a later age, Job is seeking for God where God is not. Small wonder that he fails to locate Him. Still Job is trusting in his own righteousness, not God's.

Job turns bitterly from his own helpless search for God to examine the plight of others who suffer, and the impunity with which many impose sorrow upon the poor. He begins his lament with an obscure verse, that may be translated:

> Why are not sessions of judgment set apart by   24:1
>   the Almighty,
>   and why do not they that know Him see His days?
> Some remove the landmarks;   24:2
>   they violently take away flocks, and feed thereof.
> They drive away the ass of the fatherless,   24:3
>   they take the widow's ox for a pledge.
> They turn the needy out of the way;   24:4
>   the poor of the earth hide themselves together.
> Behold, as wild asses in the desert, go they forth 24:5
>   to their work;
>   seeking prey in the wilderness as food for their
>   children.
> They reap every one his corn in the field;   24:6
>   and they gather the vintage of the wicked.
> They cause the naked to lodge without clothing;   24:7
>   that they have no covering in the cold.
> They are wet with the showers of the mountains,   24:8
>   and embrace the rock for want of a shelter.
> They pluck the fatherless from the breast,   24:9
>   and take a pledge of the poor.

> They cause him to go naked without clothing,   24:10
>   and they take away the sheaf from the hungry;
> Which make oil within their walls,   24:11
>   and tread their winepresses, and suffer thirst.
> Men groan from out of the city, and the soul   24:12
>   of the wounded crieth out:
>   yet God heedeth not their prayer.

Mention of the city suggests problems in urban life where divine justice, then as now, is completely invisible, or at least long delayed.

> There are those who rebel against the light;   24:13
>   they know not the ways thereof, nor abide
>   in the paths thereof.
> The murderer rising with the light killeth the   24:14
>   poor and needy,
>   and in the night is as a thief.
> The eye also of the adulterer waiteth for the   24:15
>   twilight,
>   saying, "No eye shall see me;" and disguiseth
>   his face.
> In the dark they dig through houses,   24:16
>   which they had marked for themselves
>   in the daytime:
>   they know not the light.

The conclusion of chapter 24 presents a serious problem for every interpreter. The meaning is clear enough, that the wicked man is carried away like a chip on the spring freshet. He does not enjoy the vineyards he has stolen. As waters evaporate, so he will go to inevitable destruction. In other words, divine justice is certain. It is difficult to picture Job uttering such thoughts at this moment. Many have decided that these words are Zophar's reply, snatched from their place and inserted here. If one is to retain these words as Job's then one must assume that they are spoken in irony, as a summary of the comforters' case that he has just demolished. Following the American Revised Version and the Revised Standard Version, I have inserted the words, "Ye say," thus making the verses a summary that leads to a sardonic con-

clusion, 24:25, in which Job savagely dares any one to show
that he is wrong and the comforters right.

Ye say: "He is swift as the waters;	24:18
their portion is cursed in the earth;	
he beholdeth not the way of the vineyards.	
Drought and heat consume the snow waters;	24:19
so doth Sheol those which have sinned.	
The womb shall forget him;	24:20
the worm shall feed sweetly on him:	
he shall be no more remembered;	
and wickedness shall be broken as a tree.	
He evil-entreateth the barren that beareth not,	24:21
and doeth not good to the widow.	
He draweth also the mighty with his power;	24:22
he riseth up, and no man is sure of life.	
Though it be given him to be in safety,	24:23
whereon he resteth,	
yet His eyes are upon their ways.	
They are exalted for a little while,	24:24
but are gone and brought low;	
they are taken out of the way as all other,	
and cut off as the tops of the ears of corn."	
And if it be not so now, who will make me a liar,	24:25
and make my speech nothing worth?	

THIRD SPEECH OF BILDAD 25:1-6

Doubtless Bildad is deeply shocked by the words Job has
spoken, yet he cannot refute them. The wicked, unhappily,
prosper, and the righteous, unhappily, suffer. But for all
the accuracy of Job's observation, his spirit is wrong, and his
conclusion, that God does not care when the righteous suffer,
is completely wrong. Likewise, Bildad starts from a right
premise and reaches a false conclusion. He sings a brief
doxology in which he stresses the thought that Eliphaz introduced early in the discussion (4:17). God is almighty. Right
premise. Man is but a worm. Whether that is right or wrong
depends upon what one does with it. If it is but a metaphor
indicating that man should be humble, Bildad is again correct. But he seems rather to mean that man is necessarily sin-

ful, hence insignificant in the eyes of God. Nothing could be further from truth.

Dominion and fear are with Him;	25:2
He maketh peace in His high places.	
Is there any number of His armies?	25:3
and upon whom doth not His light arise?	
How then can man be justified with God?	25:4
or how can he be clean that is born of a woman?	
Behold even to the moon, and it shineth not;	25:5
yea, the stars are not pure in His sight:	
How much less man, that is a worm;	25:6
and the son of man, which is a maggot?	

JOB'S THIRD RESPONSE TO BILDAD 26:1–27:23
Job retorts with biting sarcasm.

How hast thou helped him that is without power?	26:2
how savest thou the arm that hath no strength?	

The following section deals again with God's infinite, unspeakable majesty. Many commentators believe that this is a continuation of Bildad's remarks, rather than part of Job's response. Certainly it fits in with Bildad's repeated emphasis upon the divine transcendence. Certainly it is quite different from the other flashes of light that have come to Job; for the others were flashes, while this is a strong, sustained beam of light. In all the previous instances where Job has caught a glimpse of divine truth, he has plunged back into melancholy and despair. On the other hand, the song is far above Bildad's usual level of thought and expression. There is no conclusive argument one way or the other, whether this song of God's infinite power was sung by Bildad or by Job in the first edition. As it stands today, the song in all its wondrous beauty is Job's. Whoever first sang it, to me it is the most beautiful section in the Book.

The shades below tremble,	26:5
the waters and the inhabitants thereof.	
Sheol is naked before Him,	26:6
and destruction hath no covering.	
He stretcheth out the north over the empty place,	26:7
and hangeth the earth upon nothing.	

He bindeth up the waters in His thick clouds;	26:8
and the cloud is not rent under them.	
He holdeth back the face of His throne,	26:9
and spreadeth His cloud upon it.	
He hath compassed the waters without bounds,	26:10
until the day and night come to an end.	
The pillars of heaven tremble	26:11
and are astonished at His reproof.	
He divideth the sea with His power,	26:12
and by His understanding He smiteth through the proud.	
By His Spirit He hath garnished the heavens;	26:13
His hand hath formed the crooked serpent.	
Lo, these are parts of His ways;	26:14
but how little a portion is heard of Him? but the thunder of His power who can understand?	

Insofar as the book of Job presents an answer to the burning question Why, the answer is here presented. As one looks at the vast panoply of creation, one sees but part of God's work. Man cannot hope to comprehend the whole. Nature, with all its glory, beauty, and mystery, is but the whispering echo of God's voice. It does not reveal the mind of God. Only God can do that. But the man who is caught up in the grip of nature—and a crushing grip it is—can, by faith, know the Creator. Faith does not comprehend the divine plan. Yet faith knows that God reigns in the world visible and the world invisible. And, though he does not understand, the man of faith can trust.

The debate is coming to a close. The comforters have stated their case, again and again. And Job has stated his. He does not realize it yet, but with passionate sincerity he has exposed the barrier between himself and God. It is pride. "Two men went up into the temple to pray, the one a Pharisee and the other a publican. . . ." The Pharisee trusted in his own righteousness to save him. The publican looked to the mercy of God. Unlike the Pharisee, Job makes a strong case for himself.

As God liveth, who hath taken away my judgment;   27:2
  and the Almighty, who hath vexed my soul;
All the while my breath is in me,   27:3
  and the Spirit of God is in my nostrils;
My lips shall not speak wickedness,   27:4
  nor my tongue utter deceit.
God forbid that I should agree with you;   27:5
  till I die I will not remove mine integrity
    from me.
My righteousness I hold fast, and will not let it go: 27:6
  my heart shall not reproach me so long as I live.

Job is innocent of the sins Eliphaz tried to impute to him. In common honesty he cannot confess to what he has not done. Neither he nor the comforters recognizes the true barrier, pride. Of all the sins to which human nature is heir, this is the most difficult for the sinner to recognize.

Job pointedly asks how the comforters can ask him to turn to God, since they have already pronounced him a doomed sinner.

What is the hope of the hypocrite,   27:8
    though he hath gained,
  when God taketh away his soul?
Will God hear his cry when trouble cometh   27:9
  upon him?

The comforters have recited their pretty theories, Job has relentlessly exposed the unpalatable facts. Again, sarcastically, he summarizes the comforters' case:

I will teach you by the hand of God;   27:11
  that which is with the Almighty will I not conceal.

This is the portion of a wicked man with God,   27:13
  and the heritage of oppressors,
  which they shall receive of the Almighty.

The east wind carrieth him away,   27:21
  and he departeth;
  and as a storm hurleth him out of his place.

VI. THE HYMN ON WISDOM   28:1-28

    A. More elusive than gems in the mine   28:1-12

    B. More precious than gold or rubies   28:13-19

    C. Only God knows the way of wisdom   28:20-28

The Hymn on Wisdom 28:1—28

The hymn begins by singing the development of scientific technology, as symbolized by the dangerous craft of the miner who explores the dark depths of the earth, and brings forth treasure. Man can discover and utilize what is of value in the physical universe. This leads many in our day, as it led many in Job's day, to believe that the mystery of existence will respond to the same sort of searching that has discovered the sapphire (or the mystery of nuclear fission).

Surely there is a vein for the silver, 28:1
    and a place for gold where they fine it.
Iron is taken out of the earth, 28:2
    and brass is molten out of the stone.
Men set an end to darkness, 28:3
    and search out to the farthest bound
    the stones of thick darkness and the shadow
      of death.
They break open a shaft, afar from the 28:4
    houses of men,
    they are forgotten by the foot that passeth by,
    they hang afar from men, they swing to and fro.
As for the earth, out of it cometh bread; 28:5
    and underneath it is turned up as it were by fire.
The stones of it are the place of sapphires; 28:6
    and it hath dust of gold.
There is a path which no fowl knoweth, 28:7
    and which the vulture's eye hath not seen.
The proud beasts have not trodden it, 28:8
    nor the fierce lion passed by it.
Man putteth forth his hand upon the rock; 28:9
    he overturneth the mountains by the roots.
He cutteth out rivers among the rocks; 28:10
    and his eye seeth every precious thing.

He bindeth the floods from overflowing;   28:11
   and the thing that is hid bringeth he forth to
      light.
But where shall wisdom be found?   28:12
   and where is the place of understanding?

With all his fabulous technology, man has not located wisdom, though men have devoted their lives and their fortunes to its pursuit. Wisdom is not a thing, to be exposed by applying technical skill. It is not in the sea. Again we have a symbolic reference to the ocean, that suggested to Hebrew readers in another day the nature-gods of surrounding nations. Wisdom cannot be purchased with gold, jewels, or any other precious thing. Destruction and Death confess that they have heard only rumors about wisdom. Probably this is an allusion to the fantastic importance the Egyptians laid upon their funereal celebrations. At first reading, the poet seems to be saying that wisdom is more important than any earthly thing. But, since mention of these things comes bracketed between symbolic references to religious practice, one may conclude that the poet has a far deeper meaning, namely, that true wisdom comes not from religious techniques and exercises, not through extravagances of devotion, not through man's search after God, but through God's search for man.

Man knoweth not the price thereof;   28:13
   neither is it found in the land of the living.
The depth saith, "It is not in me";   28:14
   and the sea saith, "It is not with me."
It cannot be gotten for gold,   28:15
   neither shall silver be weighed for the price
      thereof.
It cannot be valued with the gold of Ophir,   28:16
   with the precious onyx, or the sapphire.
Gold and crystal cannot equal it;   28:17
   and the exchange of it shall not be for jewels
      of fine gold.
No mention shall be made of coral, or of pearls: 28:18
   for the price of wisdom is above rubies.
The topaz of Ethiopia shall not equal it,   28:19
   neither shall it be valued with pure gold.

Whence then cometh wisdom?   28:20
    and where is the place of understanding?
Seeing it is hid from the eyes of all living,   28:21
    and kept close from the fowls of the air.
Destruction and death say,   28:22
    "We have heard the fame thereof with our ears."

True wisdom is God's gift to men. It is reverence before
the ultimate Mystery, God, coupled with wholehearted obedience to the moral law.

God understandeth the way thereof,   28:23
    and He knoweth the place thereof.
For He looketh to the ends of the earth,   28:24
    and seeth under the whole heaven;
When He maketh a weight for the wind,   28:25
    and weigheth the waters by measure.
When He made a decree for the rain,   28:26
    and a way for the lightning of the thunder.
Then did He see it, and declare it;   28:27
    He prepared it, yea, and searched it out.
And unto man He said,   28:28
    "Behold, the fear of the Lord, that is wisdom;
    and to depart from evil is understanding."

VII. JOB'S FINAL SUMMARY 29:1—31:40

    A. Remembrance of happier days 29:1-25

    B. The present suffering 30:1-31

    C. Oath of clearance 31:1-40

Job's Final Summary 29:1—31:40

The cycle of debate is done. The comforters have stated their case, Job has stated his. As the debate was prefaced by a monologue, so it is followed by one, in which Job tells of his former blessedness, his present sorrow, and his claim upon God's love.

Oh that I were as in months of old,	29:2
as in the days when God preserved me!	
When His candle shined upon my head,	29:3
and when by His light I walked through darkness;	
As I was in the days of my youth,	29:4
when the friendship of God was upon my tent.	
When the Almighty was yet with me,	29:5
when my children were about me;	
When I washed my steps with butter,	29:6
and the rock poured me out rivers of oil;	
When I went out to the gate through the city,	29:7
when I prepared my seat in the street!	
The young men saw me, and hid themselves;	29:8
and the aged arose, and stood.	

Job has described the three bases of his happiness. He had the friendship of God, the love of his children, and the respect of his fellow man. He took his obligations seriously. He who was blessed tried to be a blessing to others.

I delivered the poor that cried,	29:12
the fatherless also that had none to help him.	
The blessing of him that was ready to perish came upon me:	29:13
and I caused the widow's heart to sing for joy.	
I put on righteousness, and it clothed me;	29:14
my judgment was as a robe and a diadem.	

> I was eyes to the blind,   29:15
>   and feet was I to the lame.
> I was a father to the poor: 29:16
>   and the cause which I knew not I searched out.
> And I brake the jaws of the wicked,   29:17
>   and plucked the spoil out of his teeth.

Job's relation with his neighbor grew from his relationship
with God. He lived in harmony with both. And he came in
time to believe that he had earned the right to a long, prosperous, and successful life. He had been virtuous, and virtue
is rewarded.

> I said, "I shall die in my nest,   29:18
>   and I shall multiply my days as the phoenix;
> My root shall be spread out by the waters;   29:19
>   and the dew shall lie all night upon my branch."

Though we have read his woes in revolting detail a dozen
times over, this last summary, the thirtieth chapter, has a
fresh horror all its own, as it shows the scum of society looking down upon Job. Once the elders of the city stood in his
presence:

> Now they that are younger than I have me in   30:1
>   derision,
>   whose fathers I would have disdained to have set
>   with the dogs of my flock.
>
> They were children of fools, yea, children of   30:8
>   base men:
>   they were viler than the earth.
> And now am I their song;   30:9
>   yea, I am their byword.
> They abhor me, they flee far from me,   30:10
>   and spare not to spit in my face.

Rejected by society, Job looks to heaven, and for the last
time, utters his accusation against God.

> Terrors are turned upon me: 30:15
>   they pursue my soul as the wind:
>   and my welfare passeth away as a cloud.

And now my soul is poured out upon me;   30:16
    the days of affliction have taken hold upon me.

My bones are pierced in me in the night season: 30:17
    and my sinews take no rest.

By the great force of my disease is my garment   30:18
    changed:
    it bindeth me about as the collar of my coat.

He hath cast me into the mire,   30:19
    and I am become like dust and ashes.

I cry unto Thee, and Thou dost not hear me: 30:20
    I stand up, and Thou regardest me not.

Thou art become cruel to me: 30:21
    with Thy strong hand Thou opposest Thyself
      against me.

For I know that Thou wilt bring me to death,   30:23
    and to the house appointed for all living.

When I looked for good, then evil came unto me: 30:26
    and when I waited for light, there came darkness.

My bowels boiled, and rested not: 30:27
    the days of affliction have come upon me.

I went mourning without the sun: 30:28
    I stood up, and I cried in the congregation.

I am a brother to dragons,   30:29
    and a companion to owls.

My skin is black upon me,   30:30
    and my bones are burned with heat.

My harp also is turned to mourning,   30:31
    and my pipe into the voice of them that weep.

Job's final oath of clearance, chapter 31, is magnificent in
every sense. Here in a few words have been gathered the
principles of moral conduct that fill the Old Testament. As
he surveys the past, Job is conscious of no outward action
that deserves divine censure. More than that, he has guarded
the purity of his thought. Conscious that God scrutinizes
every thought, word, and act, Job has struggled to make his
fit to offer to God.

I made a covenant with mine eyes;   31:1
    why then should I think upon a maid?

For what portion of God is there from above?   31:2
   and what inheritance of the Almighty from
      on high?
Is not destruction to the wicked?   31:3
   and a strange punishment to the workers
      of iniquity?
Doth not He see my ways,   31:4
   and count all my steps?
If I have walked with vanity,   31:5
   or if my foot hath hasted to deceit;
Let me be weighed in an even balance,   31:6
   that God may know mine integrity.
If my step hath turned out of the way,   31:7
   and mine heart walked after mine eyes,
   and if any blot hath cleaved to mine hands;
Then let me sow, and let another eat;   31:8
   yea, let my offspring be rooted out.

There follows a summary of sins to which strong men are tempted, and conjoined to the sin is a judgment upon one who is guilty. First, Job says of adultery:

If mine heart have been deceived by a woman,   31:9
   or if I have laid wait at my neighbor's door;
Then let my wife grind unto another,   31:10
   and let others bow down upon her.
For this is a heinous crime;   31:11
   yea, it is an iniquity to be punished
      by the judges.

Now comes one of the highest ethical revelations in the entire Scripture, in which Job argues that he has tried to be completely just in dealing with his servants, because both master and slave are created by God. To one who genuinely loves God, any discrimination against a fellow-man is abhorrent. It was a startling thought, in Job's day, that menials had rights. It would be a startling innovation in the twentieth century if society began acting as if the thought were correct.

If I did despise the cause of my manservant,   31:13
   or of my maid-servant,
   when they contended with me;

What then shall I do when God riseth up? 31:14
  and when He visiteth, what shall I answer Him?
Did not He that made me in the womb make him? 31:15
  and did not One fashion us in the womb?

Job has been more than just, he has been charitable. He expresses, in terms of his day, the ideal of social responsibility that must hold in a just society, whatever the date in history. He who has received much is required to show a deep, practical concern for the welfare of his neighbor who is in need. Techniques for meeting human want must vary from age to age. Job, for example, could never have dreamed of the community chest. But the response of faith to need can never change. He who loves God must be concerned about his neighbor's welfare, because such concern is a principle way of expressing one's faith.

If I have withheld the poor from their desire, 31:16
  or have caused the eyes of the widow to fail;
Or have eaten my morsel myself alone, 31:17
  and the fatherless hath not eaten thereof.

If I have seen any perish for want of clothing; 31:19
  or any poor without covering;
If his loins have not blessed me, 31:20
  and if he were not warmed with the fleece
    of my sheep;
If I have lifted up my hand against the fatherless, 31:21
  when I saw my help in the gate:
Then let mine arm fall from my shoulder blade; 31:22
  and mine arm be broken from the bone;
For destruction from God was a terror to me, 31:23
  and by reason of His highness I could not endure.

Job turns to the polite, respectable sins of desire. The first is still with us. Many today place their confidence in gold.

If I have made gold my hope, 31:24
  or have said to the fine gold,
    "Thou art my confidence";
If I rejoiced because my wealth was great, 31:25
  and because mine hand had gotten much —

The next temptation is not quite so clear to us of the twentieth century. Job refers, with revulsion, to the sun and the moon, both of which we are accustomed to admire.

> If I beheld the sun when it shined,   31:26
>   or the moon walking in brightness;
> And my heart hath been secretly enticed,   31:27
>   or my mouth hath kissed my hand;
> This also were an iniquity to be punished   31:28
>   by the Judge:
>   for I should have denied the God that is above.

He refers to sun and moon worship. When you consider that nature worship is the practical religion of many thousands in our country today, it is not surprising that in another generation the idolatrous worship of sun, moon, ocean, spring, fertility, and other natural forces and objects led many astray from worshiping God. God is Spirit. A spirit is invisible. The sun is highly visible. And it is easier to relate one's self to the visible than to the invisible. Many of Job's neighbors were sun-worshipers. Many nature cults in Job's time had an elaborate, beautiful ritual, that must have made an inevitable appeal to him. You recall how often in Hebrew history the Children of Israel went lusting after strange gods. Job, though doubtless tempted, did not yield.

All recognize the incredible difficulty in Jesus' brief command, "Love your enemies" (Matthew 5:44a). Job made a sincere effort to carry out this implication of faith in God, who is love.

> If I rejoiced at the destruction   31:29
>   of him that hated me,
>   or lifted up myself when evil found him;
> (neither have I suffered my mouth to sin   31:30
>   by wishing a curse to his soul.)

Job recalls his hospitality, famed in a land where hospitality is universally recognized as a virtue.

> If the men of my tent said not,   31:31
>   "Who can find one
>   that hath not been satisfied with his meat?"

(The stranger did not lodge in the street, 31:32
    but I opened my doors to the traveller.)

Job declares that his life has been upright; he has nothing of
which to be ashamed. He has not cowered in fear of the
crowd, nor been guilty of hypocrisy.

If I have covered my transgressions from 31:33
    men,
  by hiding mine iniquity in my bosom,
Because I did fear a great multitude, 31:34
  or the contempt of families did terrify me,
    that I kept silence and went not out
      of the door—

No further imprecation is called for, none is necessary. Job
has stated his case. He is innocent. Even yet he does not see
the flaw in his argument. He does not see that pride in his
own achievements stands between him and God. He has been
free from outward guilt. As yet he does not recognize the guilt
in his recent rebellion against God. So Job boldly declares that
he has concealed nothing; there is nothing to conceal. And
he makes his last, desperate challenge to God.

Oh, that one would hear me! 31:35
  Lo, here is my signature,
    let the Almighty answer me,
  and that mine adversary had written
    an indictment.
Surely I would take it upon my shoulder, 31:36
  and bind it as a crown to me.
I would declare unto Him the number 31:37
  of my steps;
  as a prince would I go near unto Him.

Job has unconsciously exposed the heart of his trouble.
Throughout, the chief burden has been, not the material loss,
not the sickness, and not even the loss of his children, but
Job's estrangement from God. And why is Job estranged from
God? It is largely because he insists upon marching up to
God as a prince, one proud prince greeting another and offer-
ing to correct his mistakes.

To us it seems that the defense is ended. But there follow

three verses, in which Job sings that, like a good farmer, he
has carefully tended the soil. Many critics believe that these
verses have been accidently displaced, though no textual evidence supports them. The poet long ago was not bound by
our canons of taste. Often and again he has reached a tremendous climax, and followed it by a subdued chord in a
minor key. Let us leave the verses where we find them. God
placed man in a garden and told him to till the soil. Job
has tended his farm carefully.

> If my land cry against me,   31:38
>   or the furrows thereof complain;
> If I have eaten the fruits thereof without money,   31:39
>   or have caused the owners thereof to lose
>   their life:
> Let thistles grow instead of wheat,   31:40
>   and cockle instead of barley.
> The words of Job are ended.

VIII. SPEECHES OF ELIHU 32:1–37:24

A. Introduction of Elihu 32:1-22
   1. Prose preface 32:1-5
   2. Poetic introduction 32:6-22

B. The discipline of God 33:1-33

C. The righteousness of God 34:1-37

D. Man's barriers against God 35:1-16

E. The compassion of God 36:1-22

F. The might of God 36:23–37:24

Speeches of Elihu 32:1—37:24

When the three friends have finished their consolations, and Job his defense, a new character enters the drama. This man, Elihu ("My God is He"), is one of the most maligned persons in the entire Bible. It is perfectly safe to attack him. He cannot hit back. To be sure, Elihu introduces his remarks with a recommendation of himself that is quite brash, but after that he presents the case for the comforters in the strongest and most reasonable terms that we have yet heard.

Many students today believe that the part of Elihu was not written by the same poet who composed most of the Book of Job. (This statement does not make it any less a part of God's holy Word.) The reasons given for thinking of another author are: Elihu is not mentioned in the prologue, and, even more important, in the epilogue. God rebukes only the three, in 42:7 f, but does not mention Elihu. Elihu speaks in a lower order of poetry, and a higher order of theology, than the other three. Job, who has not been exactly reticent with the others, does not respond to Elihu. In reading Elihu's speeches, you will find verbatim quotations from Job, as if he had read rather than heard what was said. And most telling of all, the language reflects a later stage of Hebrew than that in the rest of the text.

The introduction, by our standards, is almost ludicrous in its brashness. Quite possibly chapter 32 was designed as a pause to catch one's breath between Job's presentation of his right to salvation by works and Elihu's statement of God's power and glory. One gathers that the speaker does not suffer from a surplus of modesty.

> I am young, and ye are very old;　　　　　　　　32:6b
> 　　wherefore I was afraid, and durst not show you
> 　　　mine opinion.

133

> I said, "Days should speak, and multitude of years   32:7
>   should teach wisdom."
>
> Great men are not always wise: 32:9
>   neither do the aged understand judgment.
> Therefore I said, "Hearken to me;   32:10
>   I also will show mine opinion."
>
> For I am full of matter;   32:18
>   the spirit within me constraineth me.
> Behold, my heart is as wine which hath no vent;   32:19
>   it is ready to burst like new bottles.
> I will speak, that I may be refreshed: 32:20
>   I will open my lips and answer.

Having thus recommended himself highly, Elihu settles down to a business-like examination of the problem.

> Wherefore, Job, I pray thee, hear my speeches,   33:1
>   and hearken to all my words.
>
> Surely thou hast spoken in mine hearing,   33:8
>   and I have heard the voice of thy words, saying,
> "I am clean without transgression, I am innocent;   33:9
>   neither is there iniquity in me.
> Behold He findeth occasions against me, ,   33:10
>   He counteth me for His enemy;
> He putteth my feet in the stocks,   33:11
>   He marketh all my paths."
> Behold, in this thou art not just: 33:12
>   I will answer thee, that God is greater than man.

Elihu turns to the specific problem Job has raised, that God will not answer man's questions nor admit his innocence. 33:14 is obscure. Probably it means that God speaks in many ways to man. If one does not understand the first method of speaking, then God will speak in another way.

> Why dost thou strive against Him?   33:13
>   saying, "He will answer none of my words"?
> For God speaketh once,   33:14
>   yea twice, yet man perceiveth it not.

The first method by which God speaks to man is the warning dream.

> In a dream, in a vision of the night,   33:15
>   when deep sleep falleth upon men,
>   in slumberings upon the bed;
> Then He openeth the ears of men,   33:16
>   and sealeth their instruction,
> That He may withdraw man from his purpose,   33:17
>   and cut off pride from man.
> He keepeth back his soul from the pit,   33:18
>   and his life from perishing by the sword.

If man will not heed the warning dream, then perhaps God will send into his life the pain of desperate sickness.

> He is chastened also with pain upon his bed,   33:19
>   and the multitude of his bones with strong pain:
> So that his life abhorreth bread,   33:20
>   and his soul dainty meat.
> His flesh is consumed away, that it cannot be seen: 33:21
>   and his bones that were not seen stick out.
> Yea, his soul draweth near unto the grave,   33:22
>   and his life to the destroyers.

The "destroyers" are, presumably, the angels of death. When the sufferer is about to fall into their clutches, God sends another angel, whose task is to deliver him and to show him God's righteousness. The angel is but one of a thousand, so bountifully has God provided for human need. The angel serves as a mediator, both interpreting God to man and representing man before God. But more, the angel offers a ransom to God for the victim's deliverance. Possibly the ransom that Elihu has in mind is simply the chastened mood within the afflicted person. We who are Christian should always beware of reading too much into Old Testament passages. But we should likewise beware of finding too little there. Certainly Elihu did not understand the Incarnation and the Atonement as we Christians do. Should we therefore assume that the angelic mediator does not foreshadow the Christ?

> If there be an angel with him, an interpreter,   33:23
>   one among a thousand,
>   to shew unto man his uprightness;

Then he is gracious unto him, and saith,   33:24
  "Deliver him from going down to the pit;
  I have found a ransom."
His flesh shall be fresher than a child's;   33:25
  he shall return to the days of his youth:
He shall pray unto God,   33:26
  and He will be favourable unto him;
  and he shall see His face with joy;
    for He will render unto man his righteousness.

The fourth means of divine revelation is repentance. God
looks upon men, and the one who looks back to God, con-
fessing his sins, is delivered from darkness into the light.
Finally he recognizes that God's purpose in affliction is
redemptive.

He looketh upon men; and if any say,   33:27
  "I have sinned, and perverted that which was right,
    and it profited me not;"
He will deliver his soul from going into the pit,   33:28
  and his life shall see the light.
Lo, all these things worketh   33:29
  God oftentimes with man,
To bring back his soul from the pit,   33:30
  to be enlightened with the light of the living.

Elihu's defense of divine justice falls short of the ideal.
He maintains that the very nature of God is such as to ex-
clude the possibility of injustice. Yet his argument stresses
the creative might, rather than the moral character, of God.
Rightly he upholds the sustaining power of God, without
which all of the creation would return to the primordial
chaos. But the whole argument hinges upon the rhetorical
question, "Shall even He that hateth right govern?"

Today we call Elihu's type of argument "begging the question." This means assuming as true what one wishes to prove.
Job has not questioned God's government, but he is sore
troubled about God's righteousness. Elihu continues the
fallacious argument by asking, "Is it fit to say to a king,
'Thou art wicked?' " No, it is not fit, wise, or expedient to
criticize a king. But everyone knows that many kings have

been wicked, however unwise it might have been to mention the fact.

Yea, surely God will not do wickedly,	34:12
neither will the Almighty pervert judgment.	
Who hath given Him a charge over the earth?	34:13
or who hath disposed the whole world?	
If He set His heart upon man,	34:14
if He gather unto Himself His spirit	
and His breath;	
All flesh shall perish together,	34:15
and man shall turn again unto dust.	
If now thou hast understanding, hear this;	34:16
hearken to the voice of my words:	
Shall even He that hateth right govern?	34:17
and wilt thou condemn Him that is most just?	
Is it fit to say to a king, "Thou art wicked?"	34:18
and to princes, "Ye are ungodly?"	

Elihu deals more successfully with the barriers men erect against God. He shows that Job is but one of the multitude of suffering humanity who defeat their purpose by seeking the gifts of God rather than God Himself. The beasts, like men, know pain. But man ought to trust in God, as the animals cannot. When man suffers, he can know the reality of God, who enables one to sing songs in the night. This ability to see light in the darkness is a gift of divine grace. It does not for a moment negate the reality of pain, but it does enable one to transmute horror into victory. Yet man has rejected the gift because of his pride. Man refuses to accept himself as God's creature. Before the dark mystery of pain, man descends to the animal level, rejecting the grace of God which alone enables one to sing songs in the night.

By reason of the multitude of oppressions	35:9
the oppressed cry out;	
they cry out by reason of the arm of the mighty.	
But none saith,	35:10
"Where is God my Maker,	
Who giveth songs in the night;	
Who teacheth us more than the beasts of the earth,	35:11
and maketh us wiser than the fowls of heaven?"	

> There they cry, but none giveth answer,   35:12
>   because of the pride of evil men.
> Surely God will not hear vanity,   35:13
>   neither will the Almighty regard it.
> Although thou sayest thou shalt not see Him,   35:14
>   yet judgment is before Him;
>   therefore trust thou in Him.

Elihu turns again to the comforters' theme, that God is righteous, hence the righteous will prosper and the ungodly will
be destroyed. Coupled with this is his belief in the instructive
power of pain. Why does this statement of a moral law so
irritate us when we find it in Job? It is true. Evil is destroyed—finally. Good is vindicated—finally. Pain is instructive—frequently. But these happy events take place often
enough generations after the life of the one who commits the
good or evil or endures the pain. And when we read Job,
we cannot help thinking of the child who is born with a
congenital deformity, the man who, all unknowing, has mar-
ried a sexual pervert, the woman whose husband is a drunk-
ard, the parents who can visit their son only in the peniten-
tiary, the paraplegiac ward in the Veterans' Hospital.

> He withdraweth not His eyes from the righteous: 36:7
>   but with kings are they on the throne;
>   yea, He doth establish them for ever,
>   and they are exalted.
> And if they be bound in fetters,   36:8
>   and be holden in cords of affliction;
> Then He sheweth them their work   36:9
>   and their transgressions that they have exceeded.
> He openeth also their ear to discipline,   36:10
>   and commandeth that they return from iniquity.
> If they obey and serve Him,   36:11
>   they shall spend their days in prosperity,
>   and their years in pleasures:
> But if they obey not, they shall perish   36:12
>   by the sword,
>   and they shall die without knowledge.

Elihu is not smug as he confronts the reality of innocent
suffering. He bids Job and all men to recollect the law of

spiritual life, that character grows from the soil of sorrow. Those who achieve almost without exception have known intense pain. But we all know those to whom pain has brought only whimpering and despair. Elihu is closer to the heart of the mystery than were the other friends. But the mystery itself eludes his grasp. Indeed, if he could have grasped it, it would not be mystery. Humbly, before the mystery, Elihu admonishes Job, Desire not the night of death. Do not choose sin in addition to your affliction. But turn you in trust to the infinite mystery of God, whose ways man cannot comprehend.

> Desire not the night, 36:20
>> when people are cut off in their place.
> Take heed, regard not iniquity: 36:21
>> for this hast thou chosen rather than affliction.
>
> Behold, God is great, and we know Him not, 36:26
>> neither can the number of His years
>> be searched out.

Finally, Elihu contemplates the divine handiwork in nature, thus foreshadowing the thunderous climax to the Book of Job. Like Immanuel Kant, many centuries later, Elihu finds rest from his doubts in the immediate intuition of God in "the starry heavens above and the moral law within." He asks Job a series of pointed questions, to the general effect, Can you comprehend the finite works of infinite wisdom? It follows, much less can you comprehend the mystery of God's dealing with man. Elihu quite properly stands aghast at the very thought of contending with God. He believes that one who makes such a request is asking to be destroyed. Despite his inability to comprehend the infinite, he trusts in divine justice. Tragically, he ends his sermon with a sneer.

> Hearken unto this, O Job: 37:14
>> stand still, and consider the wondrous
>>> works of God.
> Dost thou know when God disposed them, 37:15
>> and caused the light of His cloud to shine?
> Dost thou know the balancings of the clouds, 37:16
>> the wondrous works of Him which is perfect
>> in knowledge?

How thy garments are warm,   37:17
   when He quieteth the earth by the south wind?
Hast thou with Him spread out the sky,   37:18
   which is strong, and as a molten looking-glass?
Teach us what we shall say unto Him;   37:19
   for we cannot order our speech by reason
   of darkness.
Shall it be told Him that I speak?   37:20
   If a man speak, surely, he shall be swallowed up.
And now men see not the bright light which is   37:21
   in the clouds;
   but the wind passeth, and cleanseth them.
Fair weather cometh out of the north: 37:22
   with God is terrible majesty.
Touching the Almighty, we cannot find Him out: 37:23
   He is excellent in power, and in judgment,
   and in plenty of justice:
   He will not afflict.
Men do therefore fear Him: 37:24
   He respecteth not any that are wise of heart.

Questions about Elihu's literary origin have obscured for
many the value in this section of Job. The general tendency
is to belittle the Elihu-portion. True, the poetry here lacks
the splendor found elsewhere in Job. However, if the Matter-
horn stood in the Himalayas, it would still be a breath-tak-
ing sight, though surrounded by far higher peaks. So the
speeches of Elihu, though surrounded by greater glories, have
a glory of their own. As A.S. Peake wisely says:

> Elihu's chief contribution is that suffering is an educative
> instrument in God's hands; it leads man to self-knowledge,
> temptation reveals to him the sin slumbering within him, which
> as yet perhaps has only failed of an opportunity. If a man
> mistakes this educative function of suffering he commits a
> grave sin and is rightly punished by God, but if he recognizes
> it and takes it to heart, suffering becomes for him a source of
> endless blessing, the highest activity of the Divine love to him.
> Cornill regards this as the highest solution open to one who
> stood at the Old Testament standpoint, for having no knowl-
> edge of a future life, he had to find an answer without passing
> beyond this life.
>   —The New Century Bible, *Job,* page 27.

The Voice from the Whirlwind 38:1—42:6

> Then the Lord answered Job out of the whirlwind. 38:1

Job has begged, again and again, for an opportunity to appear before God. Now he has it, as God speaks to him from the whirlwind. Doubtless this whirlwind belonged to the traditional prose narrative that formed the framework for the Book of Job. It was not an ordinary whirlwind. The Hebrew word denotes the setting for God's appearance at the end of the world.

The reader, like Job, expects to find Job's question answered. Why did these things happen? The question is not answered. Or rather, the answer is a long series of questions, almost all of which point directly to God's power in creation. The skeptics, to be sure, have found this quite amusing. Job asks, "Why did my children die?" and the Lord answers, "Well, have you ever seen a hippopotamus?" But Job does not find the questions amusing. While God speaks, Job comes to see himself in perspective, in a universe where all things are suffused with the light of God.

> Who is this that darkeneth counsel by words   38:2
>   without knowledge?

Job discovers that he has been darkening counsel by words without knowledge. True his words have been correct, much of the time. In all the breathtaking message from the whirlwind that follows, God says nothing that Job has not already agreed to. God proclaims His immeasurable might in creation. Job has admitted this many times over. God says that man cannot understand the ways of the infinite Being. Job has accepted this. God declares that He alone is the Ruler of the universe. Job has known it all along. Is this knowledge? Is stating the facts correctly and in logical order what one means by wisdom? No, as the Hymn on Wisdom sings:

143

The fear of the Lord, that is wisdom   28:28
   and to depart from evil is understanding.

Faith is more than accurate information about God. Faith is a personal relationship with Him. No new information is heard from the whirlwind. But the old is heard with a new reverence. There is the answer to Job's question. He gave as much of the answer as human intelligence can comprehend when he said, reverently:

Naked came I out of my mother's womb, and naked   1:21
   shall I return thither; the Lord gave, and the Lord
   hath taken away; blessed be the name of the Lord.

Many commentators have said that the Voice is speaking sarcastically to Job. I could not disagree more strongly. God, who is God, confronts Job, who is a man, and asks him to recognize the difference between man and God. Job has demanded to confront God like a prince meeting with another prince. Bildad has urged him to squirm into the divine presence like a maggot. God tells him to be a man.

Gird up now thy loins like a man;   38:3
   for I will demand of thee, and answer thou Me.

In this demand is the mystery and the miracle of faith. God, the almighty Creator of heaven and earth, enters into the I-thou relationship with man. Eliphaz has "exalted" God to such heights that He cannot notice puny beings like men. God speaks from the whirlwind to Job: I made you a man. Stand up like one. You are not a worm, you are a man, with all the glory implied in manhood. You are a man, Job, but you are not God. See yourself in perspective. You are a part of creation. As such, you cannot hope to comprehend the whole of it. But you are a part of creation of immeasurable worth to Me.

Where wast thou when I laid the foundations   38:4
      of the earth?
   declare, if thou hast understanding.
Who hath laid the measures thereof   38:5
      if thou knowest?
   or who hath stretched the line upon it?

Whereupon are the foundations thereof fastened?   38:6
    or who laid the corner-stone thereof,
When the morning stars sang together,   38:7
    and all the sons of God shouted for joy?
Or who shut up the sea with doors,   38:8
    when it brake forth,
    as if it had issued out of the womb?
When I made the cloud the garment thereof,   38:9
    and thick darkness a swaddling-band for it.
And brake up for it my decreed place,   38:10
    and set bars and doors,
And said, "Hitherto shall thou come,   38:11
    but no further;
    and here shall thy proud waves be stayed"?

This allusion to the sea must be understood both in a literal
and a symbolic sense. Literally, God has established sea and
dry land. The geologists say that as long as there has been
ocean, there has been land. Continental boundaries come
and go, but continents remain. Anyone with half an eye can
watch shore-lines changing under the impact of wave erosion.
But the destructive force of the sea has not been able to
destroy the great land masses. The Lord reminds Job, and
us, of this fact, which is at the least remarkably convenient
for the continuance of human life. But in a symbolic sense,
God reminds us of something even more important. The sea,
throughout the Book of Job, has served as a symbol for
evil. Almost every reference suggests Babylonian mythology,
in which the sea was the primaeval enemy of God. In a
symbolic sense, then, God tells Job and us that the force
of evil, always present in the world, can never be totally
victorious. During our lives on earth we must engage in a
never-ending struggle against the powers of darkness. But as
we struggle, we must remember always that God has established limits beyond which evil cannot go.

Briefly now the Voice alludes to God's moral purpose in
creation, using another picturesque figure of speech. The
earth lies asleep, under a blanket of darkness. Then the
dawn, at God's command, grasps the corners of this blanket
and shakes the wicked from it like dust. Thus light checks
the lawless plans of evil men.

> Hast thou commanded the morning since thy days;   38:12
>   and caused the dayspring to know its place;
> That it might take hold of the ends of the earth,   38:13
>   that the wicked might be shaken out of it?
> It [the earth] is changed like clay under a seal,   38:14
>   and it is dyed like a garment.
> And from the wicked their light is withholden,   38:15
>   and the high arm shall be broken.

In a bewildering succession of queries, the Voice asks Job about the incredible diversity and glory of creation.

> Hast thou entered into the springs of the sea?   38:16
>   or hast thou walked in the search of the depth?
> Have the gates of death been opened unto thee?   38:17
>   or hast thou seen the doors of the shadow of death?
> Hast thou perceived the breadth of the earth?   38:18
>   declare if thou knowest it all.
> Where is the way where light dwelleth?   38:19
>   and as for darkness, where is the place thereof,
> That thou shouldest take it to the bound thereof,   38:20
>   and that thou shouldest know the paths
>   to the house thereof?
> Knowest thou it, because thou wast then born?   38:21
>   or because the number of thy days is great?
> Hast thou entered into the treasures of the snow?   38:22
>   or hast thou seen the treasures of the hail,
> Which I have reserved against the time of trouble,   38:23
>   against the day of battle and war?
> By what way is the light parted,   38:24
>   which scattereth the east wind upon the earth?
> Who hath divided a watercourse for the over-   38:25
>   flowing of waters;
>   or a way for the lightning of thunder;
> To cause it to rain on the earth, where no man is;   38:26
>   on the wilderness, wherein there is no man;
> To satisfy the desolate and waste ground;   38:27
>   and to cause the bud of the tender herb
>   to spring forth?
> Hath the rain a father?   38:28
>   or who hath begotten the drops of dew?

Out of whose womb came the ice?   38:29
   and the hoary frost of heaven,
     who hath gendered it?
The waters are hid as with a stone,   38:30
   and the face of the deep is frozen.
Canst thou bind the sweet influences of Pleiades,   38:31
   or loose the bands of Orion?
Canst thou bring forth Mazzaroth in his season?   38:32
   or canst thou guide Arcturus with his sons?
Knowest thou the ordinances of heaven?   38:33
   canst thou set the dominion thereof in the earth?
Canst thou lift up thy voice to the clouds,   38:34
   that abundance of waters may cover thee?
Canst thou send lightnings, that they may go,   38:35
   and say unto thee, "Here are we?"
Who hath put wisdom in the inward parts?   38:36
   or who hath given understanding to the heart?
Who can number the clouds in wisdom?   38:37
   or who can stay the bottles of heaven,
When the dust groweth into hardness,   38:38
   and the clods cleave fast together?

Turning from the mystery of material creation to the deeper mystery of life, God asks again:

Wilt thou hunt the prey for the lion,   38:39
   or fill the appetite of the young lions,
When they couch in their dens,   38:40
   and abide in the covert to lie in wait?
Who provideth for the raven his food?   38:41
   when his young ones cry unto God,
   they wander for lack of meat.

Knowest thou the time when the wild goats   39:1
   of the rock bring forth?
   or canst thou mark when the hinds do calve?
Canst thou number the months that they fulfil?   39:2
   or knowest thou the time when they bring forth?
They bow themselves,   39:3
   they bring forth their young ones,
   they cast out their sorrows.

Their young ones are in good liking,   39:4
    they grow up with corn;
    they go forth, and return not unto them.
Who hath sent out the wild ass free?   39:5
    or who hath loosed the bands of the wild ass?
Whose house I have made the wilderness,   39:6
    and the barren land his dwellings.
He scorneth the multitude of the city,   39:7
    neither regardeth he the crying of the driver.
The range of the mountains is his pasture,   39:8
    and he searcheth after every green thing.
Will the unicorn be willing to serve thee,   39:9
    or abide by thy crib?
Canst thou bind the unicorn with his band   39:10
    in the furrow?
    or will he harrow the valleys after thee?
Wilt thou trust him, because his strength is great?   39:11
    or wilt thou leave thy labour to him?
Wilt thou believe him,   39:12
    that he will bring home thy seed,
    and gather it into thy barn?
Gavest thou the goodly wings unto the peacocks?   39:13
    or wings and feathers unto the ostrich?
Which leaveth her eggs in the earth,   39:14
    and warmeth them in the dust,
And forgetteth that the foot may crush them,   39:15
    or that the wild beast may break them.
She is hardened against her young ones,   39:16
    as though they were not hers:
    her labour is in vain without fear;
Because God hath deprived her of wisdom,   39:17
    neither hath He imparted to her understanding.
What time she lifteth up herself on high,   39:18
    she scorneth the horse and his rider.
Hast thou given the horse strength?   39:19
    hast thou clothed his neck with thunder?
Canst thou make him afraid as a grasshopper?   39:20
    the glory of his nostrils is terrible.

He paweth in the valley,   39:21
    and rejoiceth in his strength:
    he goeth on to meet the armed men.
He mocketh at fear, and is not affrighted;   39:22
    neither turneth he back from the sword.
The quiver rattleth against him,   39:23
    the glittering spear and the shield.
He swalloweth the ground with fierceness   39:24
    and rage;
    neither believeth he that it is the sound
    of the trumpet.
He saith among the trumpets, "Ha, ha!"   39:25
    and he smelleth the battle afar off,
    the thunder of the captains and the shouting.
Doth the hawk fly by thy wisdom,   39:26
    and stretch her wings toward the south?
Doth the eagle mount up at thy command,   39:27
    and make her nest on high?
She dwelleth and abideth on the rock,   39:28
    upon the crag of the rock, and the strong place.
From thence she seeketh the prey,   39:29
    and her eyes behold afar off.
Her young ones also suck up blood: 39:30
    and where the slain are, there is she.

After ranging wide through the realm of created animals, that God has made, not Job, the Voice from the Whirlwind asks:

Shall he that contendeth with the Almighty   40:2
    instruct Him?
He that reproveth God, let him answer it.

Job will no longer contend with God. He is speechless with awe, in the presence of divine omnipotence. Job was not the creator of heaven and earth, God was and is. Job admits that he can make no reply:

Behold, I am vile; what shall I answer Thee?   40:4
    I will lay mine hand upon my mouth.
Once have I spoken; but I will not answer;   40:5
    yea, twice; but I will proceed no further.

This was not God's aim in speaking to Job. For Job to clap
his hand over his mouth and keep rebellious thoughts from
being spoken is really no gain. What is accomplished if
divine power has stunned a person into silence? God desires,
not Job's silent rebellion, but Job. He does not ask for a
shrunken caricature of Job, one who is of small account in
his own eyes, and resentful because of it. God wants Job;
his love, his time, his talents, his all. So He continues:

> Gird up thy loins now like a man: 40:7
>   I will demand of thee, and declare thou unto Me.

Clutching his own righteousness, Job has again and again
denied that God is righteous. And the Voice from the Whirlwind asks, infinitely sad:

> Wilt thou also disannul My judgment?   40:8
>   wilt thou condemn Me, that thou mayest be
>   righteous?

The answer, writ large in human history, is YES, man will
condemn God to bolster his high opinion of himself. The
hands of men, not devils, nailed Jesus to a cross. Adam and
Eve in the Garden were tempted, "Ye shall be as gods" (Genesis 3:5), and therein lay the cause of their fall. Similarly,
Job has condemned God through pride in self.

God is not proud. He is willing to stoop and accept us
proud mortals. He stoops now to Job and asks him, in
imagination, to sit upon the divine throne and execute justice
upon earth. Job has been a critic. Could the critic take the
divine Author's place? Obviously not. Then how can he,
who cannot even in imagination do God's work, tell whether
or not God is doing it well?

> Hast thou an arm like God?   40:9
>   or canst thou thunder with a voice like His?
> Deck thyself now with majesty and excellency,   40:10
>   and array thyself with glory and beauty.
> Cast abroad the rage of thy wrath: 40:11
>   and behold every one that is proud,
>   and abase him.
> Look on every one that is proud,   40:12
>   and bring him low;
>   and tread down the wicked in their place.

Hide them in the dust together;	40:13
and bind their faces in secret.	
Then will I also confess unto thee	40:14
that thine own right hand can save thee.	

Job's question is not answered. But now it is clear to him that the answer lies in a realm where human wisdom cannot follow. He has rediscovered the elemental truth that man is not God.

Underlying every criticism of God is an unspoken assumption. In the twentieth century people usually assume that God should have arranged the world so that man will be comfortable. If this were the divine purpose, then any one can see that He has missed the mark. But we who are Christian, far more than Job of old, should be able to see that God's mysterious purpose is achieved in the valley of the shadow. We find the focal point for Christian faith upon a Cross, a monstrous, horrible, bleak tragedy. This Cross, which seems to man the ultimate denial of divine sovereignty, is the power of God unto salvation. We do not understand the Cross of Christ. It is a mystery. But the mystery is aglow with heavenly light, the same light that Job now sees shining through the darkness.

Job's sickness is just as painful as it was before God spoke. The loss of his flocks and herds still rankles, just as it did before. The hollow emptiness caused by the death of the children is still hollow. But there is a difference. Where before Job has rebelled, he is beginning again to accept.

Since Job does not respond, the Voice continues, asking about two more of God's creations, behemoth (the hippopotamus) and leviathan (the crocodile). Most critics believe that yet another author composed these sections. The scholars are divided in their understanding of the creatures, whether the poem refers to mythical animals or the living creatures. In ancient Egypt, the two were associated frequently both in the Nile valley and in many religious mural frescoes. In late Hebrew thought, the two had a decidedly mythological significance. It is said that they were created on the fifth day of Creation, to be the food of the righteous in Messianic times. Hence, we are dealing with flesh and blood animals that had a mystical connotation. The flesh and blood animals were frequently captured, but these in the poem defy capture. The Voice calls Job's attention to these creatures of God, and asks, If you do not dare face these created things, how can you dare to face their Creator?

> Behold now behemoth, which I made with thee;   40:15
> he eateth grass as an ox.
> Lo now, his strength is in his loins,   40:16
> and his force is in the navel of his belly.
> He moveth his tail like a cedar: 40:17
> the sinews of his stones are wrapped together.
> His bones are as strong pieces of brass;   40:18
> his bones are like bars of iron.
> He is the chief of the ways of God: 40:19
> He that made him can make His sword to
> approach unto him.
>
> Can any take him by his eyes?   40:24
> Or pierce through his nose with a snare?
>
> Canst thou draw out leviathan with a hook?   41:1
> or press down his tongue with a cord?
> Canst thou put an hook into his nose?   41:2
> or bore his jaw through with a thorn?
>
> Canst thou fill his skin with barbed irons?   41:7
> or his head with fish spears?
> Lay thine hand upon him,   41:8
> Think upon the battle, thou wilt do so no more.
> Behold to hope for him is in vain: 41:9
> shall not one be cast down even at the sight
> of him?
> None is so fierce that dare stir him up: 41:10
> who then is able to stand before Me?

In what seems a mere parenthesis within the vivid description of leviathan, the poet expresses God's answer to Job's insistent demand. Job has thought that his righteousness constituted a claim upon God's justice. But now he hears that no gift in man's power to offer is enough to put God under obligation. Man is saved, not through his skill at practicing religious exercizes, but through the fact that God is love.

> Who hath given Me a gift that I should repay him?   41:11
> Whatsoever is under the whole heaven is Mine.

The thought is irritating to the modern mind, that God is the Author of man's salvation, not man. The thought likewise irritated Eliphaz, Bildad, Zophar, Elihu, and Job. Today this idea is associated with the name of John Calvin, who is an unpopular thinker because he expressed it with considerable vigor. To be sure, some Calvinists have affirmed in revolting ways that God is Author of salvation. But the thing expressed is the essence of New Testament teaching, however inept some interpretations may have been. Indeed, the Apostle Paul may well have been echoing Job when he wrote, "Who has given a gift to Him that he might be repaid?" (Romans 11:35, RSV.) Toward the end of the Scripture, divine love says, "Behold I stand at the door and knock" (Revelation 3:20). It is not our task to bang at the door to get God's attention; it is our task to open the door, locked by pride, and let Him in.

Christianity is not a variety of magic to force obedience from a reluctant deity. It is a response to divine love, a stern, austere love that sometimes leads us through the valley of the shadow, that led Job to the ashes, that led Jesus to the Cross. Why do these tragedies occur? I do not know. But this I do know. When finally we are able, like Job, to look at human problems from the divine perspective, we shall thank God for every tear we have shed on earth.

If the translation given is correct, then 41:11 is the second of two pivots upon which the entire Book of Job hinges. The first, of course, is the Satan's cynical question in 1:9. However, as often has been the case, the most meaningful verses are the subject of most dispute. Candor compels one to acknowledge that the Septuagint, translated two or three centuries before Christ, reads:

> Who has assailed Me and been safe   41:11
> since everything under the heaven is Mine?

Most modern translators agree that the Septuagint is mistaken in making the verse under discussion a mere parallelism with 41:10.

The poet returns to his fascinated examination of leviathan. This is one more instance where a tremendous emotional climax is followed by what seems to us an anticlimax. But we must remind ourselves again that the standards of today were not the standards of ancient Israel. The Voice is intent upon depicting the fierce leviathan. So the picture continues:

> The sword of one that layeth at him cannot hold;   41:26
>   the spear, the dart, nor the habergeon.
> He esteemeth iron as straw,   41:27
>   and brass as rotten wood.
> The arrow cannot make him flee: 41:28
>   slingstones are turned with him into stubble.
> Darts are counted as stubble: 41:29
>   he laugheth at the shaking of a spear.
> Sharp stones are under him: 41:30
>   he spreadeth sharp-pointed things upon the mire.
> He maketh the deep to boil like a pot;   41:31
>   he maketh the sea like a pot of ointment.

Job, like the reader, has lost all interest in crocodiles. His rebellion is ended. He is not merely stunned into silence. He repents. He confesses none of the sins that Eliphaz tried to impute to him; for of these he was guiltless. His sin lay in making judgments about matters that he could not understand.

In humiliation Job paraphrases the words that God has spoken to him (38:2, 3.) He sees now that he has arrogantly been ordering God about, making demands upon Him, rather than waiting patiently for the Lord. He confesses that his faith has been second-hand, by the hearing of the ear. He has received much theological instruction, words about God, not God. But now, he says, "Mine eye seeth Thee." This expression cannot be taken literally. It means that Job is fully conscious of God's presence, and by divine light he has come to see Job clearly. If you will examine your Bible carefully for examples of the divine-human encounter, you will find in every instance that the one who meets God is overwhelmed with fear. So with Job. In the presence of Him who is fully righteous, one's human arrogance looks hideous and revolting.

> I know that Thou canst do every thing,   42:2
>   and that no thought can be withholden
>   from Thee.
> "Who is he that hideth counsel without   42:3
>   knowledge?"
>   Therefore have I uttered that I understood not;
>   things too wonderful for me, which I knew not.
> I have said: "Hear, I beseech Thee,   42:4
>   and I will speak:
>   I will demand of Thee
>   and declare Thou unto me."
> I have heard of Thee by the hearing of the ear;   42:5
>   but now mine eye seeth Thee:
> Wherefore I abhor myself   42:6
>   and repent in dust and ashes.

Earlier Job has made himself of small account. Now he abhors himself. (The Hebrew word implies "melting into nothingness.") But God will not have it so. At the moment of salvation, Job discovers that he is a sinner. Reverse the statement. When Job sees himself in perspective as a creature who has rebelled against his Creator, and the shame of his rebellion pours in upon him, then he is saved.

Job suffers still, not as a punishment for his sin; for the sin came after the sorrows began. He has no intellectual explanation for his suffering, nor have I. But he knows again that he can trust God. A deep, personal fellowship with Him is possible once more. He knows that his pain has played a part in God's plan of salvation. Though he cannot explain what part, he realizes that God knows, God cares, and God permits human sorrow only that some good greater than the sorrow may result. The last tremendous climax in Job has come. It is his humble acceptance, "Thy will be done" (Matthew 26:42b).

Epilogue in Prose 42:7-17

When Job has answered the Voice from the Whirlwind, the poem comes to an end and the prose epilogue begins. The Lord speaks wrathfully to the three comforters. Elihu, significantly, is not mentioned. God says that they have not spoken "the thing that is right," as Job has done. Indubitably, the comforters have spoken many right things about God, and Job has said many false things. Yet God rejects their pious platitudes, and accepts the man who has dared to think.

To us, the size of the burnt offering required of the three friends is almost incredible. An offering of seven bullocks and seven rams was ordained for the entire nation's sin. (See Ezekiel 45:22-25.) Such a sacrifice on behalf of three individuals is staggering. But they made the sacrifice, and Job interceded for them. You recall that the only Old Testament mention of Job, outside the Book that concerns him, shows him as a master of intercessory prayer. (See Ezekiel 14:14f.) During the lonely days on the ash-heap, how often had the comforters prayed for Job? Good advice they offered in plenty. Why did they forget to pray?

> And it was so, that after the Lord had spoken these 42:7
> words unto Job, the Lord said to Eliphaz the
> Temanite, "My wrath is kindled against thee, and
> against thy two friends: for ye have not spoken
> of Me the thing that is right, as My servant Job
> hath. Therefore take unto you now seven bullocks 42:8
> and seven rams, and go to My servant Job, and of-
> fer up for yourselves a burnt offering; and My serv-
> ant Job shall pray for you; for him will I accept:
> lest I deal with you after your folly, in that ye have
> not spoken of Me the thing which is right, like My
> servant Job." So Eliphaz the Temanite and Bildad 42:9
> the Shuhite and Zophar the Naamathite went and

> did according as the Lord commanded them: the
> Lord also accepted Job.

The following verse may tell us much or little about the
date when the Book of Job was written.

> And the Lord turned the captivity of Job, when   42:10a
> he prayed for his friends.

The expression "turn the captivity" is a Hebrew idiom meaning "restore to prosperity." The idiom did not rise in a
vacuum. It would be only natural that such an idiom should
develop during a period of captivity. The use of the phrase
may be a suggestion—certainly it is nothing more—that the
book was composed during or shortly after the Hebrew
captivity in Babylon.

The concluding words prove, for many, among the most
troubling in the entire book.

> Also the Lord gave Job twice as much as he had   42:10b
> before.

One major purpose of the book is to refute the idea of material
retributive justice. And now, when Job has learned that
God is his Treasure, he finds himself flooded with earthly
treasures once more.

Though we are not specifically informed, the sickness must
have ended. The gifts pressed upon Job were symbols of
friendship, of no great monetary value. His enrichment, we
presume, was accomplished the hard way, by painstaking
attention to the details of ranch life. The number of his
flocks and herds was doubled. The number of his children
was the same. It has been suggested that, since the Book
of Job indirectly states the case for believing in eternal life,
the number of Job's children also is doubled, for those readers
who are willing to accept the full implication of the fact
that God is love.

> Then came there unto him all his brethren, and   42:11
> all his sisters, and all they that had been of his
> acquaintance before, and did eat bread with him
> in his house: and they bemoaned him, and com-
> forted him over all the evil that the Lord had

brought upon him: every man also gave him a
piece of money, and every one an earring of gold.
So the Lord blessed the latter end of Job more   42:12
than his beginning; for he had fourteen thousand
sheep, and six thousand camels, and a thousand
yoke of oxen, and a thousand she-asses. He had   42:13
also seven sons and three daughters. And he called   42:14
the name of the first Jemima [dove], and the name
of the second Kezia [cassia], and the name of the
third Kerenhappuch [horn of eye paint]. And in   42:15
all the land were no women found so fair as the
daughters of Job: and their father gave them inheritance among their brethren. After this lived   42:16
Job an hundred and forty years, and saw his sons,
and his sons' sons, even four generations. So Job   42:17
died, being old, and full of days.

There is an often-encountered explanation for the mysterious ending. The explanation runs that the Joban poet
took a traditional narrative as the framework for his examination into the ways of God with man. As the narrative begins
with a theological conundrum, namely a mutual agreement
between God and the Satan, so it ends with another theological puzzle, the bringing of material retributive justice
to one who has already discovered that the reward of faith
is God, not any of God's gifts. One who deals with a tradition is bound by its terms. As Tennyson had no choice but
to name King Arthur's sword Excalibur, so the Joban poet
had no choice but to include God's puzzling agreement with
the Satan and the happy ending. In any case, there is a
profound element of symbolic truth in the naive simplicity
of the old folk story. As there is in human life an unex-
plained element of evil; so there is in human life an unex-
plained element of reward. Those who know God and keep
His commandments know far more inward security, happiness,
peace of mind, and true success than do those who ignore
or despise God.

The explanation does not explain. It is just a little too
facile to be convincing. The Holy Spirit has led the Joban
poet, and the reader, through many dark and devious ways to
express the truth that God is light. In the course of the poem,

the author has demonstrated his freedom from human convention again and again. This man, whose hands and mind God untied, was not fettered to a tradition. When he concludes the book with a happy ending, he is expressing a profound and important truth, not just retelling an ancient story. We have seen that the Joban poet expresses some of his strongest arguments as parentheses in the discussion of something else. Some of his major conclusions have been stated by indirection. So it is not surprising that the significance of the happy ending lies beneath the surface; nor is it surprising that many have failed to find that significance. The conclusion of Job, like so much else in the book, is a puzzle that many theologians have failed to solve. But a poet in our time, Archibald MacLeish, has presented the solution with a clarity that I have found nowhere else.

> Job is given all he had before twice over—all but his children who are the same in number but more beautiful. And that is not all. Not only is Job *given* his life again: Job *accepts* his life again. The man who was once highest and happiest and has now been brought lowest and made most miserable; the man who has suffered every loss, every agony, and for no reason, moral or intelligible, the mind can grasp; the man who has cried out to God for death, begged over and over to die, regretted the womb that bore him, yearned never to have been, never to have breathed the air or seen the light—*this* man accepts his life again, accepts to live his life again, take back his wife again, beget new children mortal as those others, risk himself upon the very hazards on which, before, his hopes were wrecked. And why? Because his sufferings have been justified? They have not been justified. God has merely lifted into the blazing fire of the imagination His own power and Job's impotence; His own immeasurable knowledge and Job's poor, trembling, ridiculous ignorance. Job accepts to live his life again in spite of all he knows of life, in spite of all he knows now of himself, because he is a man... Man can *live* his truth, his deepest truth, but cannot speak it. It is for this reason that love becomes the ultimate human answer to the ultimate human question. Love, in reason's terms, answers nothing. We say that *Amor vincit omnia* but in truth love conquers nothing —certainly not death—certainly not chance. What love does is to affirm. It affirms the worth of life in spite of life. It affirms the wonder and the beauty of the human creature, mortal and insignificant and ignorant though he be. It answers life with life.
>
> —*"About a Trespass on a Monument," New York Times,* Sunday, December 7, 1958.

Appendix

It is almost an axiom among students of Job that his disease was elephantiasis. Since, through no fault of my own, I have had the dubious privilege of examining several victims of elephantiasis, I cannot go along with the majority. The symptoms I have seen do not seem to me to resemble closely those described in Job. When I read the Book looking for actual physical symptoms, I was quite surprised to find how few are mentioned, and to discover the number of physical metaphors for spiritual pain. For example, I believe 16:13 to be such a metaphor. Recognizing that almost all will disagree with some of my inclusions or exclusions, I submit the following as the verses describing Job's sickness: 2:7; 3:24, 26; 6:7; 7:5, 14; 9:17, 18; 16:8; 17:7; 19:17, 20; 30:15-19, 26-30. After you have reread these verses, contrast your findings with a clinical description of elephantiasis.

ELEPHANTIASIS

In filarial elephantiasis, there occur attacks marked by severe systematic disturbance, with *elephantoid fever*. Following or accompanying this, the affected part becomes inflamed, swollen and tender, often with more or less oozing of clear milky serum. The attacks are recurrent, and vary considerably in duration, frequency, and severity. Following each exacerbation, however, the affected part is sensibly increased in size, until finally it may assume enormous proportions. There may be 10 to 20 or more attacks in a year, and after each the swelling and induration are greater, although the fever and general disturbance are less with each succeeding exacerbation. The skin is at first edematous and doughy, and pits on pressure; but, as a result of long continued inflamation, it becomes hardened and indurated and may assume a rugose appearance. Chronic dermatitis often results from the decomposing secretions, and, in cases of long standing, ulceration is common. During intervals, the symptoms, aside from the pain which results from weight and pressure, are remarkably trivial. The progress of the disease is slow but progressive. Although the

condition may affect only one part, the involvement may be
quite extensive and even general.
   The degree of hypertrophy varies greatly. There may be
only moderate hyperplasia of the skin and subcutaneous tis-
sues, with dilation of the superficial lymphatics and more or
less oozing during the exacerbations; or the increase in size
may be enormous.

—Richard L. Sutton and Richard L. Sutton, Jr.,
Diseases of the Skin, page 1317.

In contrast with the poetic descriptions scattered through
Job, the above clinical description sounds almost cheerful.
There certainly are similarities. Perhaps 7:5 (see Revised
Standard Version) has led some to a degree of assurance that
I do not share. In the medical text, ulceration comes at an
advanced stage, but in Job the boils mark the onset of his
illness. Elephantiasis gains its name from the hypertrophy,
which may be truly elephantine. But in Job there is no
evidence of hypertrophy, except possibly 30:18. However, in
16:8 and 17:7 one discovers that wasting away is a principle
symptom. The presence or absence of hypertrophy is not
conclusive, but its absence should suggest further investiga-
tion.
   My medical adviser tells me that when a patient is referred
to him with an "atypical" this or that, his first thought is
always that he is dealing with a wrong diagnosis. If Job had
elephantiasis, it was an atypical case. Accordingly, I present
two more diseases, both of which are suggested by Peake, and
another proposed in The Interpreters' Bible.

ORIENTAL SORE

Goodall (1937) described 63 cases occurring in British troops
after the Quetta earthquake of 1935; some 12 percent of the
men, healthy on arrival, developed the disease. They were
bitten by sandflies. A small sore would appear as a reddish
papule, which increased gradually in size. After a number
of months it would become bluish in the center, soften and
ulcerate. There was no pain or itching, although in Indians
such lesions regularly became secondarily infected. The number of lesions ranged from 1 to 17, and was most often 3 to 8;
single sores were rare. At its complete development the ulcer
may be several centimeters in diameter. It is surrounded by
an infected zone in which one may find numerous parasites.
After a duration of several months or even a year, an un-

treated ulcer undergoes cicatrization and leaves a characteristic undelible scar.

−*ibid.*, pages1287–1288.

Job's scraping his sores with a potsherd was a sure invitation to secondary infection. If he suffered from Oriental Sore, it was a complicated case, since an uncomplicated infection produces no intense itching or burning. In 7:5 and other places Job mentions parasites. Their presence certainly is not conclusive, one way or the other.

ECTHYMA

Ecthyma is an acute inflammatory disease, characterized by the formation of one or more discrete, flat, pea to fingernail size pustules, which may be followed by slight scarring or temporary pigmentation. Both children and adults are attacked. The legs and thighs are the sites of predilection, although no region is exempt. The lesions which vary in number from 1 to 20 or more, are usually circular or irregularly oval in outline and sharply defined, with pinkish or reddish areolae. They begin as small, yellowish, pustular excavations, which enlarge by peripheral extension. In 10 to 14 days they begin to desiccate, and soon dry up, forming thick, adherent, brownish crusts. The bases are excoriated and raw, and tender on pressure. There is considerable induration. The crusts drop off within a few weeks, although the disease may be continued indefinitely by the development of new lesions. In the mild type of the affection, ecthyma simplex, there usually results some temporary brownish pigmentation, but no scarring. In severe and deeply seated examples, ecthyma gangraenosum, scarring is the rule rather than the exception. The lesions give rise to itching and burning at times, and there may be some accompanying systemic disturbance.

−*ibid.*, pages 912–913.

PEMPHIGUS FOLIACEUS

Large, fragile, flaccid bullae develop rapidly. They contain pus from the first. They soon rupture, usually at some marginal point, leaving a moist, raw surface covered with seropurulent fluid. The eruption involves the entire surface in the majority of instances... There is a diminution of the adhesion between the stratum corneum and the subjacent prickle layer... The crusts may be thin and adherent, but usually they are thick and easily detached. The foul smelling pus in which they are constantly bathed imparts to them a peculiar, distinctive, sickening odor. The involved mucous surfaces are denuded

and raw, and in severe cases the hair and nails may be ex-
foliated. The skin is infiltrated and quickened. As a rule the
subjective symptoms are comparatively trifling. The course of
the disease is essentially chronic. Exacerbations, followed by
periods of comparative quiescence, are common, but the skin
seldom clears between attacks.

—ibid., page 343.

It seems to me that more of Job's symptoms are described
under the clinical heading of Ecthyma than any of the others.
Pemphigus foliaceus is a strong contender, while Oriental Sore
and Elephantiasis fight it out valiantly for last place.

From my extended browsing in *Diseases of the Skin,* I have
emerged with two major conclusions.

1. Long range diagnosis is an unrewarding task.

2. Certainty in diagnosis would not enhance the value of
reading Job.

Pain presents its own spiritual problems that seem, in many
instances, quite unrelated to its source. There are two types
of pain that Job did not experience. He did not suffer as a
direct result of his own sin, and he did not know the agoniz-
ing shame that comes through a trusted person's betrayal.
As I have been urging my friends in Christ to read the Book
of Job, I have found that the most meaningful expressions of
gratitude come from those who are enduring the last named
variety of pain.